Memories of My Childhood in 1940's Wenlock

BY JANET PREEN-JONES

ISBN:

With grateful thanks To my husband, Garvin,

my rock for the past 62 years

And all my wonderful family

This book is printed in black and white. However, many of the photos are originally in colour

If you wish to view them in colour, please go to my Website www.janet-preen-jones.com/amazing-places/Memories-of-Childhood-pix

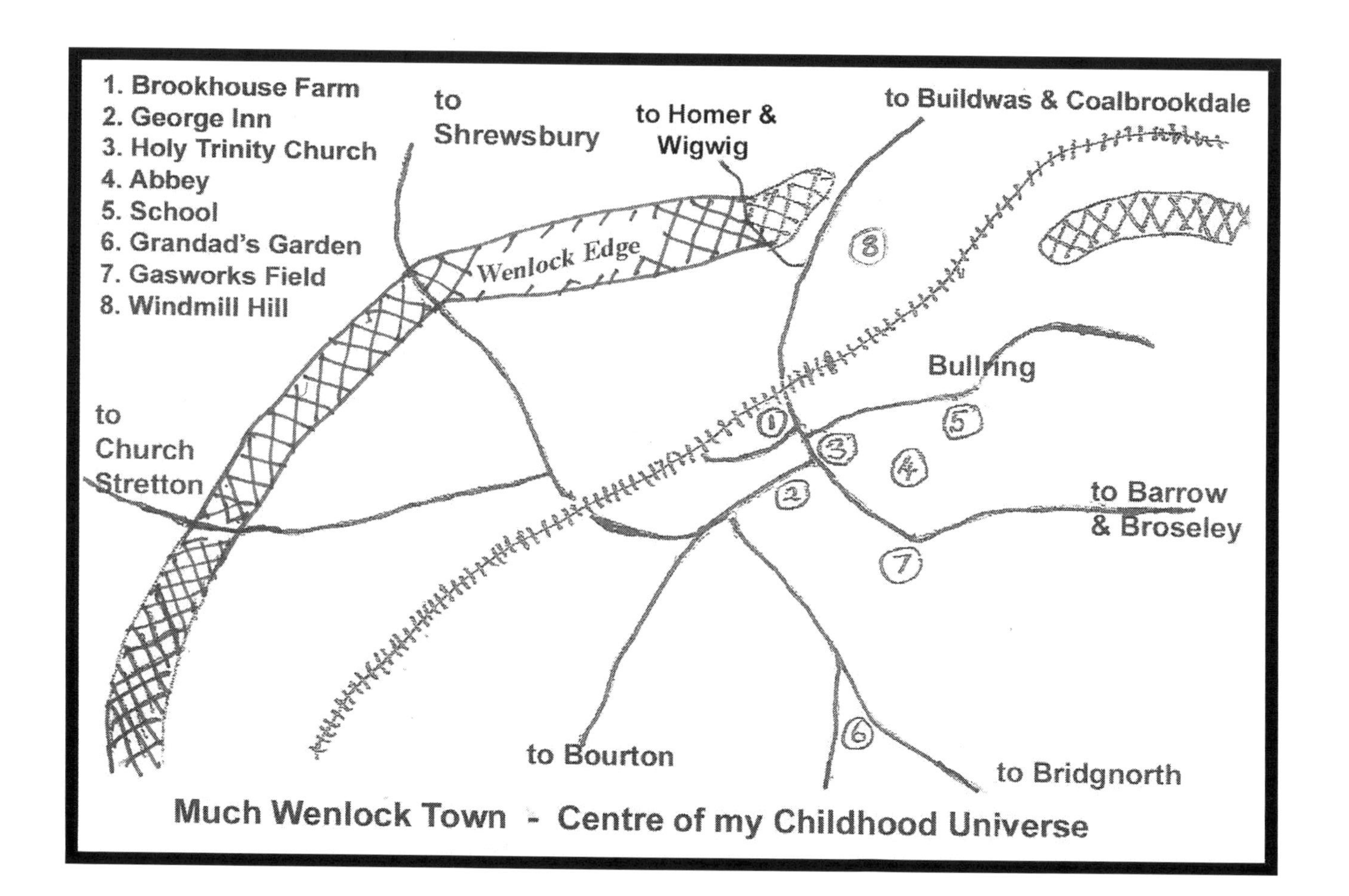

Much Wenlock Town - Centre of my Childhood Universe

Introduction

I was born in the little town of Much Wenlock, Shropshire, UK In June 1936 and these stories represent a kaleidoscope of treasured memories from the first 15 years of my life. Naturally, I do not remember much about the first 3 years although the odd perception of falling out of my pram haunted me for years! Imagine my surprise when my first attempts to apply lipstick revealed a slight scar on my lip.

"Mum, where did that come from?" I asked.

"Oh! That happened when you fell out of your pram when it got away from Mary (our 14year old maid) and tipped over! Is it still there? I had forgotten all about it," Mum chuckled, "I was really cross with her at the time. I think you were about 18 months old.".

Since my Mother ran the dairy and looked after the Poultry, (including hatching her own chickens and turkeys), as well as Household chores and looking after three children, Mary was an essential part of our pre-war lives.

The 1940's were a decade of disruption, shortages, isolation, and tremendous change for Britain. The Education Act of 1944 which took effect in September 1946, raised the school leaving age to 15 and extended the 'scholarship for Grammar School' opportunity to all. From 1946 onwards all children who would be 10 or 11 on July 31st sat the entrance exam for Grammar School. Although, like all systems, it had its faults it did mean that I was fortunate to spend my Grammar School years, constantly challenged and stretched by the brightest and most inquiring minds among my peers.

I grew up in a world and homelife of constant change! By the time I reached 16 I had lived in four homes, attended four schools, yet still my home area remained Wenlock and my constant anchor The George Inn and Grandad Yates. In those days, of necessity, we accepted the 'slings and arrows of outrageous fortune" picked up the pieces and carried on!

Pleasure and happiness lie in making the best of what you have and appreciating the unexpected! It cannot be measured by worldly wealth and possessions. All too frequently, an over-attention to such matters is more likely to breed despair and resentment.

I think back with enormous gratitude to my Mother, who lived this maxim though some extremely difficult years. Her ability to find pleasure in small things, to always look for the window of opportunity and above all never to give up was extraordinary.

I hope you enjoy my ramblings as I have enjoyed recording them! To those of you who also lived in the 1940's these are my memories; others may have different recollections. We all view the world from our own unique perspective and, to some extent, selective memory. I trust these stories will trigger many happy recollections of your own childhood world!

1. A Turning Point

I held tightly to Uncle Bob's hand as I walked along the top fence-rail. It was September 2nd. 1939 and I was 3 years and nearly 3 months old.

The branches of the trees standing along the fence were loaded with golden plums creating a rich contrast to the damson trees lining the driveway. Their branches were already drooping with masses of damsons all coated with that magical bluish sheen that could be rubbed off with a small finger to reveal the shining purple skin. Alas the taste was usually sharp and slightly sour, but I loved damson jam best of all.

Two days before, Daddy had brought us to visit Aunty Elsie and Uncle Bob at their farm 'Poiselands' just south of Birmingham and we were to stay several days. Daddy and my older brother, Bryan, went back after lunch as they had to be home in time to start the milking on our own farm.

At 8 years old Bryan loved helping Dad around the farm and couldn't wait to be off! So, with hugs and calls of "See you next week," they were soon away.

Aunty Elsie was my mother's oldest sister. She was always so happy to see us and we loved her dearly. Aunty Elsie made time to talk to us and really listened to all we had to say. Alone among our aunts, Auntie Elsie never told us to be quiet and sit still like good little girls!

Instead, she would dig in her cupboard for an old biscuit tin filled with a collection of characters or trinkets which had all been saved from freebies in cereal packets or discarded toy sets. We loved the golliwogs which had been attached to Robertson's marmalade jars best of all. This collection kept my sister and I busy for hours.

Uncle Bob was special too. He was such fun to be with, opening our eyes to so much beauty in the countryside around us as we accompanied him on his tasks around the farm. But above all he talked to us as equals, something that was extremely rare in those days.

On their small farm, they kept large numbers of chickens, just one cow for milk, a litter or two of young pigs and some ducks. Much of the chicken feed was home grown and as were the potatoes. Harvested potatoes were put through a 'Riddler' which allowed all the smaller ones to fall through and saved the larger ones for sale in the market. Those that fell through were boiled and fed to the pigs.

The large kitchen garden and orchard supplied vegetables and fruit. On Thursdays they loaded up their little Austin 7 car and drove to Bromsgrove where they had a 'Round' serving a large group of regular customers. This round also provided an outlet for their eggs and chickens and fresh pork and beef, when available. Aunty Elsie also sold her home-made jam and pickles. Many regular customers drove out to the farm for their supplies on the weekend.

When the plums, damsons, greengages, and apples ripened there was far too much to sell to their regular customers. If we visited during fruit season, we could join them once or even twice a week on a trip to one of the local produce markets. Here the baskets of fruit were laid out in groups along the pavement and sold by auctioneer to the local shopkeepers.

My sister and I had been looking forward to this planned visit for several weeks. But our first full day had been very strange with everyone clustered around the wireless to listen to Mr. Chamberlin telling us that we were at war with Germany. I did not know what war meant exactly but I knew that it made grownups afraid for the future and brought back dark memories of the past.

Mum cuddled us both as our older cousins (Joyce was thirteen and Leslie eleven) talked to their father and mother and all of them tried to make some sense out of what might happen. Uncle Bob had been in the Army in France for the whole of the 1st World War. Some years later he told me that at one point they were so hungry that they ate the bark from the trees!

My Father had been a soldier too although, since he did not turn 18 until September 1918, he never served overseas, and our Mum was afraid that he might have to serve again. Today she was especially worried because we were away from home. The pervading gloom among the adults hung over us all!

But now I was enjoying the glory of my fence walk and seeing the world from a new perspective! I was keeping my happiness extremely quiet! Any unusual sound would alert my mother to glance in my direction. Inevitably I knew that the result would be a frantic scream to Uncle Bob.

"Get her down Bob. She's too young for that!"

Sometimes that phrase seemed to be the story of my life!

So, with one ear open for her screech of protest, I was enjoying being the tallest in my small world for the first time and I was loving it.

The expected scream did come, not from Mum but my sister and it was a scream of delight!

"Look, look", she cried "Its Bryan and Daddy".

She had seen my brother opening the road-gate at the end of the long driveway and waiting for Daddy's car to turn in

Our big old black Vauxhall bumped up the lane, between two fields of golden wheat and then we were all running across the orchard to meet them. My older brother Bryan was bouncing up and down in the front seat half hanging out the window as he waved and hollered. But the strangest thing was that they were pulling the black high-sided box trailer and inside was a large squealing pig!

Mum was so pleased to see them she was crying tears of joy as they rolled to a stop. In those days, telephones were few and far between and there had been no way for Daddy to tell us he was coming. But I knew that the grownups had been extremely concerned as everyone was supposed to stay off the roads and not travel.

Mum had been very worried about being away from home at such a time. Consequently, his unexpected arrival was a big relief for the adults but tinged with sadness for my sister and I for we realized our holiday was about to be cut short!

The pig was making more noise than any of us as he voiced his rage at his unexpected jaunt across Shropshire and into Worcestershire. Daddy explained that his official excuse for the trip was to deliver a pig to his brother-in-law, but, since no one had stopped them to question the trip, his excuse for the journey home would be the collection of a pig he had bought from Uncle Bob! But we must pack up quickly for the journey home, as he had to be back for milking.

Mum rushed upstairs to pack whilst Joyce helped Susan and me to change into our best dresses and cardigans for the journey home.

Then Joyce packed our small suitcase as we hunted around to make sure nothing was forgotten. We helped her add our few toys, I think there was a bear and Susan insisted on carrying Jane, her large rag doll.

When we returned to the living room, everyone was waiting for us and it was clear there were to be no special treats from Aunty Elsie, but Mum was clutching a bag which smelled sweet and spicy.

"No food before your journey, it may make you carsick. But your Mummy has some treats for when you get home" she whispered.

Carsickness was a common occurrence with most families in those days. It was not surprising really when you consider we bounced around in the large back seat with no safety devices other than a strap hanging from the roof near the door. The roads wound around and around in never ending tight curves and were frequently almost too narrow for two cars to pass. In addition, we children travelled most of the way either standing up or kneeling on the seats for a better view.

After a quick cup of tea, (yes, even small children drank weak tea in those days,) and many hugs and kisses and some tears from Mum and Aunty Elsie, we were quickly on our way home. Little did I realize at that time that it would be many years before I was to see my favourite aunt and uncle again.

2. My First Home

Home for us in 1939 was the Brookhouse Farm in Much Wenlock. It was one of several farms and Smallholdings which were based within the town. In contrast, all the farmland was scattered around the surrounding countryside. We had fields down the Bullring, on the Broseley road, up the Sytche Lane and above the Sytche Coppice, (the 'Top Ground'), along the Farley road, above the cemetery and the Windmill Hill itself. Our biggest field was 'the Broad Meadow' which stretched from the Windmill Hill to Station Road (also called the Slang). This field is now the site of William Brookes School.

Parts of the house and Farm Buildings date back to medieval times, even the 'modern' addition is already several hundred years old. Perched on the corner of Queen and Sheinton streets we saw the Church and the Guildhall on Wilmore Street with Dodd's Shop on the corner of the Bullring. Other windows and the front door faced onto Sheinton Street with the Police Station immediately opposite.

Milking time meant a long walk to bring in the cows, and another long walk to take them out again. Since all the town farms were in the same situation virtually every road was splattered with new and old cowpats! Horses were still widely used and contributed to road 'furniture' with enthusiasm. Rose lovers frequently sallied forth armed with bucket and spade to collect the horse manure which was a preferred (and highly prized) fertilizer!

We still had 4 or 5 cart horses but only one tractor, a fairly recent purchase. An old steam lorry was parked in the stackyard sheds alongside steam rollers and other remnants of the Road Construction side of my Grandfather's business (a casualty of the great depression of the 30's).

Harvesting beets on the sloping field beyond the Windmill Hill. Wilfred the Horse Boy with my father, Don, and my sister alongside. This field no longer exists! Its location is now beneath the huge Quarry Pool known as the 'Blue lagoon locally.

My Father was up every morning at 4.45am. as the milk had to be ready for pickup by the CO-OP lorry by 7.30am. I would often wake in total darkness to the distant sounds of the cows being herded home by our faithful old English sheepdog, Nell. The cacophony increased to an ear-splitting roar as they passed beneath our bedroom window and into the yard beyond.

One morning I decided to get up and help! Imagine my dismay when my astonished father packed me back off to bed with a stern warning to stay put until Mum called us.

1946:Bryan with Trooper and Ben ready for work.

One facet of a town farm was the large midden heap (one of several about the town) which grew steadily with every cleanup after milking etc. We were used to the background odour and paid little attention except during manure spreading season.

This odorous job was carried out whenever there was a lull in other farm chores during late autumn to early Spring. Remember that almost everything was done manually in those days.

This meant the men had to stand on the hardened parts of the pile (uncovering the more pungent softer interior) and throw forkfuls into the waiting cart, a disturbance which significantly magnified the already strong aromas!

When fully loaded the horse and cart headed to the chosen field and the men, once again standing on the pile, scattered the manure either side as the horse was led across the field. This provided fertilizer for the next year's crops. Yes, we really were organic in those days!

Getting rid of the whole pile sometimes seemed to take several weeks and really stirred up the smell! It was certainly 'hold your nose' time until the job was finished, and the pile settled down to rot in peace!

Every time one of us was sick and Dr Bigley was called, he never failed to stop at the landing window and look out on the manure pile in disgust.

"You will never raise healthy children Mrs. Yates as long as they live with that!"

Inside the Brookhouse itself all the floors were on the same level between the old and 'new' parts of the house. However, the floor of the whole house (we had no basement) was a good six inches lower than the street on both sides and even more below the backyard! The only exceptions were the back kitchen and the toilet which were recent additions two steps up from the main floor. They had concrete floors and corrugated iron roofs.

The only flush toilet was in this small 'room' sticking out from the side of the house into that narrow space between the Brookhouse and the new terraced houses on Sheinton Street. It seemed to have been built at the same time and on the same level as the back kitchen. This meant that it was two steps up to the lavatory door also, which made it especially difficult for short people like me to open the door! Like the back kitchen it had a roof skylight but there was no window. There was a small window alongside the back door in the back kitchen.

One momentous day I found that I could finally reach the sliding lock whilst inside the toilet and promptly locked the door! Alas, locking it was one thing, unlocking was beyond me! My screams for help brought the family and lots of advice and sco2dings but all to no avail.

Eventually Jack Langford, our cowman, then a youthful red-haired teenager, was called away from the milking on a rescue mission. He climbed up onto the roof of the back kitchen and crawled across it to the small lavatory skylight above my head. Fortunately, as usual it had been left slightly open and, with considerable squirming he was able to shimmy down to my rescue. He was my hero for evermore!

Our front door was shorter than most with a big step down into the hall. Most people had to duck their heads and my grandfather who was at least 6 ft 6 inches had to positively stoop! It was up steps from the Back Kitchen to the back yard too.

As a small child, whenever I was sent to answer the either the front or back door, I found it very disconcerting to have to crank my neck back for ever just to identify a face that was suddenly very much higher than it should have been.

At that time, the house was divided into two sections. Great Uncle Henry lived in the oldest part nearest the farmyard. His door, sheltered by a small porch and low wall, opened onto our backyard. A big 'box' of panelled wood which enclosed his staircase protruded into Mum and Dad's bedroom. We could sometimes hear him thumping up and down the stairs and grumbling to himself.

Henry was Granddad Yates' younger brother. When I was small,

I did not realise he was related to us. I knew that Granddad Yates saw that he was looked after and that someone brought his dinner down from the George every day. But I don't believe he went much further than the yard and he had few visitors. I never heard him speak pleasantly to anyone, even my father who was his nephew.

Henry seemed to hate us children and always appeared to yell at us to keep quiet when we played on the yard outside our back door. His ancient oak door would fly backwards with a mighty bang and out he would hobble cursing and swearing at us and waving one of his crutches wildly. We were all afraid of him and we felt no sadness when he died, I think it was in 1943.

Poor Henry had no friends, he had offended everyone. Mum told me his story as an example of what harm is done when a mother spoils her youngest child and denies him nothing. Henry had been very wild when he was young and quickly became an alcoholic. In theory he was the bailiff for the Brookhouse farm, (at that time still rented by his Aunt Alice Yates-Ainsworth) but in fact he spent most of his time and energy drinking and partying.

After his father died in 1892 his mother could deny him nothing and in a few short years they brought the family businesses to the brink of bankruptcy.

One-night Henry had fallen down the stairs while he was drunk and broken his leg! Even when it mended, he remained very lame and got about with crutches. Now he officially could not work! Had it not been for his drinking he could perhaps have helped by serving in the bar at the George, but this was out of the question. He would have drunk more than he sold!

We kids always thought of him when we sang the old nursery rhyme on rainy days, thoughts which probably increased our volume and enthusiasm!

"It's raining, it's pouring, the old man is snoring,

He went to bed and bumped his head

And couldn't get up in the morning."

It seems we had a nursery rhyme to sing for every occasion in those days!

3. Our Town During the 1930's and 1940's

In 1939 and for the next ten years Wenlock remained, as it had been for centuries, a very self-sufficient little town! The coming of the railway in 1850 had provided a sturdier link to the outside world, however the latter remained an optional and useful service, to be used when useful rather than a source of change to the timeless pattern of centuries.

The celebrated author, Mary Webb who spent her childhood in Much Wenlock referred to it as 'a very rip van winkle of a town that had fallen asleep sometime in the Middle Ages!

However, as the centre of the oldest and largest Borough in England, we 'Wenlockians' regarded our town as the 'Capital' of our area!

Most of us had been born in Wenlock itself, or within a few miles and families were so intertwined that at least half the population were related by blood or marriage.

In fact, Wenlock was 'town' for most of the surrounding farms and villages. The Farmers Market on Smithfield was a busy place almost every Monday. And, although our street market no longer operated, Wenlock provided a wide choice of shops for every need.

Today, when all Supermarkets carry a huge selection of fresh produce and processed food from all over the world it seems incredible to look back on a time when almost all our needs were supplied fresh from local sources!

As with most towns across Britain the ravages of the deep recession of the 1930's had resulted in a few empty store-fronts. However, most businesses continued to hang on, living on the edge of poverty, really having no alternative means of support. Frugality was a way of life, waste an abomination!

In such a world, self-respect, pride and respectability assumed enormous importance! These were the symbols of success. Money and position were accepted facts over which we had little control.

Almost everyone rented their property from the Abbey Estates and rents were frozen throughout the War and for many years after. I believe the rent collector visited the cottages weekly, but all businesses and farms paid their rent in person at the Gaskell every Quarter Day.

Looking back, it is amazing to think of the amount of control exercised by landowners. Even in 1950, when my mother wished to purchase land from the estate to build a house, the sale was not permitted until Mrs. Ward (the then current owner of the Abbey Estates), had reviewed the Architect's drawings, and deemed that our new house met with her approval!

Some of the most coveted houses were those built by the Council in the 1920's – The Crescent, Southfield Road and Havelock Crescent! All these houses had front and back gardens, indoor plumbing, and full bathrooms, plus electricity! Many of the older houses and most of the cottages did not! No one had central heating; we relied on coal fires for heat and often for cooking too!

Gardens or allotments provided a major contribution to our diet and nothing was allowed to go to waste! I remember my mother putting out the word that our thirteen blackcurrant bushes were ready and loaded with berries. All were welcome to come and pick, but please leave a picked basket for her! By noon, the next day the bushes were picked clean!

The war brought additional hardships, especially for those still suffering from WW1 injuries! Men who had lived through the horrors of one war and WW1 widows who had battled to raise a family alone had to watch their sons being taken to fight yet another war! The youngest veterans of WW1 found themselves re-called to their old regiments!

Thinking back to my childhood it amazes me how many women had jobs in addition to running the house and caring for the children. Most of the smaller shops were run by women, their husbands (if they had one) were employed fulltime in other trades or in the Military. Women made up the vast majority of teachers and all the nurses!

Many widows and single women ran their own small holdings raising chickens and a few sheep, goats and/or beef cattle. Often, these women had just carried on after the death of their husband or parents. Others worked as 'char ladies' (cleaning ladies) helping to bridge the gap created by the exodus of all the young unmarried girls to better paying jobs in the munitions factories. The land army brought city girls to live and work on the larger farms. Some stayed on after the war preferring the country life to smoky cities!

Mum, Susan and Bryan with Christmas turkeys

We often talk of the huge loss of life in WW1 and see the long lists of the 'Fallen' on old Memorials. We do not often think of the fact that each of those men killed was either the husband or future husband of some poor woman who, despite Society's perceptions regarding women, had to find a way to survive and often raise a family in a world where a 'working woman' was often viewed with suspicion and became 'faceless' as a social entity!

4. Shopping Day, Our Special Treat

Accompanying Mum on her Friday afternoon shop in Wenlock was a big treat! This was very much a social outing calling for clean dresses and freshly braided hair! Mother herself wore her 'best' clothes with her favourite hat and handbag. She even put on a dab of powder and smear of lipstick!

Primarily a social event, lots of time seemed to be spent waiting patiently while Mum met with friends and neighbours. We were always certain to meet several farmers' wives in from the countryside around as well as most of the members of the WI and Mothers' Union! This was a time to catch up on all the village gossip and discussing upcoming events and plans without giving one's complete commitment! Such conversations always ended with

"Well of course I'd love to but I'm not sure, I'll have to check with my husband"!

It was fascinating to hear how my mother's way of speaking would immediately change from 'Kings English' to broad Shropshire (and visa versa) to match her audience. Since we were always corrected unless we spoke 'properly' this seemed a bit unfair! In her defence, looking back now, I don't think she was even aware of the way her speech changed.

Christian names were never used! It was always 'Mrs. Yates'. Since there were several 'Mrs. Yates' in and around the town, when mentioned in other folks' conversation, their husbands' Christian name would be added. In Wenlock, we had Mrs. Don Yates, Mrs. Ted Yates, and Mrs. George Yates in our family alone!

Our first stop was always Phillips Grocery Store. Here, as in most stores, there were chairs in front of the counter where the ladies always sat as they gave their order. The shop assistant quickly came forward with a small order pad, (on which she wrote Mum's name and the date), and a cardboard box. Very few items were pre-packaged, everything had to be weighed or cut so it was quite a lengthy process. Mother would request 2lbs of sugar. This would be written on the order pad, weighed carefully, tipped into a blue paper bag, added to the box and the price written on the order pad. Next it was the tea. I think the flour came in 2 lb bags ready packed and of course there were some tinned items like syrup, baked beans and canned fruit which used 'points' from our Ration Books. There was no frozen food!

The cheese wheel was massive and a special marble slab with a cutting wire was used to cut off the requested amount. If it weighed too little Mother would request that they cut again. I suppose the other piece was sold to another customer. When rationing started the amount had to match our ration allowance and inevitably included a small slice added to make the weight exactly. Coffee beans were weighed and then ground, filling the air with their pungent aroma.

Flitches of bacon hung from the roof on huge hooks and these were lifted down and cut by Mr. Martin himself. Mr. Martin was the manager and there was another younger man was the Assistant Manager. All the machines were operated by these two men. The shopgirls only wrote and packed the orders and did all the cleaning and shelf stocking.

When our order was finally finished, the order list was placed inside the box which was set on one side ready for the Delivery Boy. He had a bicycle with a huge basket and often he had already delivered our order before we returned home. Nobody locked their back door and delivery people just came in and set stuff on the table inside the back door.

Now it was time to pay for last week's groceries. Mother had brought the previous week's list with her having checked all the prices and amounts carefully when she unpacked the box. If there were any discrepancies these were discussed and rectified. Only then did she take out her purse. Susan and I became very attentive at this point waiting for our favourite part!

The bill and the cash were placed by the shop assistant in a small metal cup. This cup was pushed into the base of a long tube. Immediately with a tremendous whoosh the cup shot up the tube and over our head down into a small glassed-in box which was about 2 feet higher than the shop floor. Here sat a very stern old lady with glasses perched on the end of her nose. She stamped the bill paid, made a note in a huge register, put any change required in the metal cup and 'whoosh' back it came to our assistant. This apparatus was considered to be very 'modern' or 'new-fangled'!

Our next stop was the Butchers. Clayton and Graingers shop was in Raynalds Mansions, an extremely large beautiful old black and white house with huge windows and even its name carved into the decorative design! The half door was always open, and a strong breeze blew throughout the long narrow shop area towards the open back-half door to their backyard. It seemed a big step down onto the red quarry tile floor which was liberally covered with sawdust! The very air was redolent with the smell of meat! Sides of lamb, pork, beef, strings of sausages, unplucked chickens, furry rabbits and, in season, partridge and pheasants hung headfirst from nails behind the counter.

Mr. Warburton, I remember him as being very tall and thin and wearing a large blue and white striped apron over a white jacket, towered behind the butcher block counter as he wielded his axe awfully close to my nose. The glassed-in display counter contained a sparse display of joints which had already been cut, pork and lamb chops, pork and beef sausages, black pudding sausages and large pans of tripe. I have never tasted tripe, the look of it and knowledge of its origin were sufficient to place it on my 'never ever' list along with my father's favourite, poached brains'!

Mum needed to choose the Sunday joint! We usually had lamb or beef. Her choice was made with much deliberation. Only rarely would she accept one from among those in the glass case. She preferred a freshly cut joint where she could inspect its source!

Usually, Mr. Warburton would lift down a side of beef or lamb onto the big butcher block just level with my nose! I hastily skidded backwards through the sawdust as a couple of blows from his axe reduced the side to halves or quarters. One piece stayed on the block; the rest were rehung on the large hooks along the wall behind the counter.

With our Mum giving precise instructions, he used a long sharp knife to cut a joint to fit her requirements! An exceedingly small square of greaseproof paper separated the meat from the scales! A small bill tag (about the size of a credit Card) with the weight, price and our name was slapped on top and speared onto the meat with a curly ended pin. The curl held the price ticket safely during later delivery. Our meat went into a large blue and white enamel tray with all the other orders. The delivery boy would carry several orders in his large basket on the front of his bicycle with no additional wrapping.

Saying 'Goodbye' to Mr. Warburton we trailed behind Mum into the next room to where old Mrs. Grainger sat behind the iron grill window of her tiny room within a room! As usual we did not pay for today's purchase but for the previous week's orders. It seemed to take forever to check the amount owing and finally hand over the money. Everything was paid in with cash. Meat was generally bought as needed and Mother would have popped up during the week to buy sausages, scrag end of lamb or liver to supplement the Sunday roast. We had rabbit stew whenever my Father managed to shoot one, but we never bought rabbit.

It was a huge thrill if we needed to visit the treasure-trove of Formby's hardware! That dimly lit, low ceilinged little shop seemed such a massive step down from the street through one narrow half of the double door. The whole interior was packed to the rafters with everything anyone ever dreamed of. Small items such as nuts and bolts, washers, nails, and screws came in bulk and were sold by weight. Dad would ask Mum to pick up such items. For anything larger he came himself!

Often there were shoe repairs to be collected from Mr. Jones, the Cobbler, or a call at the Chemist for Andrews Liver Salts or Syrup of Figs (the latter a weekly Saturday night routine). Mrs. Connell opposite the Guildhall sold everything from lino to buttons. and her son, Pat Connell, was the only Electrician in town! Her large sign protruding onto the narrow street read

'Charles Edwards' and it was many years before I learned that this was her father's name.

Wilmore Street, Brook House in the distance.

Our last stop was always at Thompsons the Newsagents on Barrow Street. Our daily newspaper was delivered each morning, but the bill was always paid at the newsagents during our Friday afternoon shopping trip. If we were especially good Mum might buy us some crayons or a new pencil! By Summertime those we had received in our Christmas stocking were virtual stubs. Alas, any reminders usually met the same reply "Nonsense there's plenty of use left in them yet!

By the time we arrived home it would be teatime. 5pm was teatime! There would be a plate of bread and butter and a dish of jam with weak milky tea to drink, some variety of fruit pie, perhaps jam or syrup tart and either a Victoria sponge or a cut and come again cake. If the weather was very cold, sometimes we would be allowed to toast our bread in front of the fire before it was buttered. It was considered unwise for children to have a heavy meal before bed. I have no recollection of my father being there at teatime. I expect he ate later.

Bedtime was 6.30-7 pm with no exceptions. Mother would read us a short story, hear our prayers, tuck us in with a goodnight kiss and woe betide anyone who made a sound after that! As my brother grew older, he could stay up a bit later. In the spring and autumn, when dusk came earlier than high summer, he often went with Mum and Dad to shut up all the henhouses at dusk.

5. The Old Corner Shop

The tiny black and white cottage squeezed between the Churchyard and the Bullring has been established there for many centuries. Will we ever know who built it, or even the reason for its location. Was it an addition to the old stone stable (now a house) next door or did the little house come first? Who added the little hexagonal room?

Certainly, it has survived many centuries and many tenants. During most of the 19th century it seems to have been a tailor's home and business. Perhaps the little hexagonal room was added on for the first tailor who set up shop there. In 1841, the Tailor was William Bailey, in my Grandfather's youth, (he was born 1861) it was the home and business of William Hammond and his family. Grandad remembered Mr. Hammond sitting cross-legged on his worktable in the middle of the little room surrounded by windows! With only candles for extra light, having sufficient natural light was essential for a tailor! I imagine that his grandstand view of everything going on in the town brightened his day immensely!

When I was a little girl it was and had been for many years, Dodd's Sweet Shop! Whenever we looked out towards the Church from our home at the Brook House Farm, Dodd's Shop sat stoically on the Bullring corner as it had for centuries. My brother remembered when the old stone building alongside was one of our farm stables and held five horses! But in the 1940's it was just an empty shed where the Dodd's kept their coal. By then, although we still had several carthorses, an Allis Chalmers tractor had reduced their number considerably!

Every Thursday evening after tea Dad did his accounts and calculated the amount of money required to pay the men and buy their Insurance Stamps. The cash required plus any required for household expenses was drawn from the bank each Friday morning. In those days Banks were only open from 10am to 3pm.

My father made up the wage packets on Friday evening. I loved to 'help' with this job. My duties included counting out the change for each wage package and sticking the Insurance stamps on each card. The reward, which was shared between my sister and I, was the excess blank sticky paper which was torn from the sheet of stamps. This was our only source of sticky paper and was valued like gold!

Saturday was payday. The workers drifted into the dairy just after 12.30pm and indulged in some general discussion on the week's activities before formally lining up in order of seniority to be paid. I think that almost all the men had worked for my father or grandfather since leaving school at fourteen. We three children stood at the end of the line! As the youngest, I was always last, a position I grew used to over the years!

Dad ceremoniously set everything out on the dairy table. He brought his big ledger with him and each man had to check their pay and sign for it. It was a formal occasion! First the hours were checked, then the tax deductions which were re-calculated using large Tax Table books. Dad had already calculated this, but occasionally, some of the men, unhappy with the amount deducted, would want to make sure that everything was correct. They were also shown their Insurance card and initialed the stamp to confirm the card had been stamped for that week. Finally, the prepared pay envelope was opened, and the money was counted out.

It seemed to take forever as we three kids hopped up and down waiting for our turn!

Jack, the last workman in line, was in his early teens and helped to pass the time. He always had time to tease and joke with us 'younguns'. In fact, he was nearer to our age than to the other men all of whom were over fifty at least.

Eventually, after some general discussions which ranged from farm activities to current news, the men were on their way and it was our turn. Bryan, being ten years old, was paid a whole sixpence; Susan and I got threepence. After one penny had been posted into our moneybox, we set our two pennies on the sideboard until after dinner.

It seemed an eternity until we were released to go spend our 'pay'!

The only door into Dodd's house opened into their Living Room/Kitchen. The top half of this door was open unless the weather was very bad. It provided additional light to the living room for the small deep window wells were filled with plants and surrounded with heavy curtains. After politely knocking on the half-door, we lifted the latch and stepped into the family living-room. This room was dominated by a large table in the centre. It was draped in a dark tapestry cover that almost reached the floor. Sometimes their two children, who were in High School, were sitting at the table reading or doing homework. Once they were sorting and counting ration coupons and it looked like fun!

Mrs. Dodd was generally busy at a big black iron range which ran along the side wall. Dressed in black, frequently wearing a black shawl around her shoulders, with swollen legs and feet squeezed into carpet slippers, she never had a smile. It was a good day when she acknowledged our entry with a grunt, more frequently it was "wipe your feet!"

Mr. Dodd had been injured in the First World War and still moved very slowly with a limp. He had lost his arm as well. All he had left was a stub about four inches long to which he strapped a long-tapered cylinder of polished wood. This was about six inches long and he had learned how to manipulate it to wedge things between his stump and his body.

With a grunt, Mr. Dodd slowly rose from his wooden rocking chair beside the fire and led us into the tiny hexagonal shop. To me, that small room was Aladdin's cave! A high counter with a flap to allow Mr. Dodd access was built across the centre of the room. Behind the counter (which was way above my head), jars of candy stood in glittering splendour along the shelves. One line of jars could be seen from the street; those below revealed only the tantalizing thick coloured screw tops of hidden joys. Higher up above the window were tins of tobacco and cigarettes. A continuous line of Advertisements, mostly for cigarettes, decorated the walls just below the ceiling. A single light bulb hung down over the counter.

The chocolate bars and special candy like fudge and Edinburgh Rock filled the shelves lining the wall to the Mr. Dodd's left. Below these the left side of the counter itself was crammed with opened boxes of 'junk' candy such as liquorice pipes, candy cigarettes, marshmallow ice cream cones, sherbet fountains and lollipops. (There was no chewing gum in those days.)

A set of balance scales graced the right end of the counter. These were special candy balance scales with tiny brass weights piled ready beside the flat side and a funnel shaped brass dish set on the other. On the wall above tiny white cone shaped bags, not much bigger than an ice-cream cone, and small white square bags, each pack threaded though with a loop of string, dangled from nails. I don't remember seeing a cash register. I think the cash was kept in a box under the counter. When rationing started Mr. Dodd kept the scissors to clip the coupons and the box of carefully saved tiny coupons under the counter too

Watching him weigh and package our sweets was fascinating. First, he lifted the big, sweet jar to the counter with his good arm and removed the lid. Next the correct weights were placed on one side of the scale. Now, with his arm around the large jar and the wooden stump balanced against the rim, he poured exactly the right amount into the scale pan. Only rarely did he need to use his good hand to remove any excess. After opening the bag into a cone shape, he tucked it between his wooden stump and his body and tipped the sweets from the scale into the bag. Replacing the scale dish, he deftly twisted into a screw the paper top of the bag and pushed it across the counter.

The poor man must have found our agony of indecision extremely trying. He knew exactly how much we had to spend and how little return would be left for themselves. But I never heard him raise his voice or try to hurry us along. On the rare occasions that Mrs. Dodd took his place, we knew we had to make up our minds very quickly and forgo the joys of indecision until Mr. Dodd was well enough to return to his place behind the counter. She was not averse to the terse words or scathing comments which I often felt were really intended for our parents.

My favorite choice was 'Hundreds and Thousands' and 'Jelly Babies'. My two pennies would buy an ounce of each. Tipped into individual tiny cone shaped bags, I felt the joys of plenty as I pushed my two pennies across the counter. I knew that if I ate them very very slowly I could make them last almost until teatime. You see, some Hundreds and Thousands are like tiny Liquorice Allsorts with the liquorice strips replaced with coloured sugar paste strips. It is possible to peel one strip off at a time and then let them melt on your tongue for the longest time. But the Jelly babies went quickly! There was always a risk that Susan or Bryan would finish their choices and beg a taste of mine. But I knew they thought Hundreds and Thousands were babyish and beneath their notice so I made those last as long as I could!

Occasionally, Mr. Dodd had trays of toffee! It seems strange to think of it today when everything is individually wrapped, but Mr. Dodd's wartime toffee came in small tin trays about eight inches by seven inches. The toffee was a solid block about ¼ inch thick and scored into small squares. The scored lines did not completely break through the toffee. In fact, often they were barely more than indentations.

I loved to ask for toffee just to watch Mr. Dodd take his tiny toffee hammer to tap carefully until the toffee broke into small pieces. He would hold the tray down on the counter with his wooden stump and wedge himself against the counter to keep the tray still. If course that old toffee never broke along the indented lines! It would shatter into shards between a few larger chunks!

This was OK by me for I loved to eat the tiny shards very slowly and always asked Mr. Dodd to give me the little pieces! When all the toffee was sold there were always two or three teaspoons of powdery residue, almost dust, on the little tin trays. I wonder! Did his own children have that scattered over their spotted Dick and Custard?

When wrapping paper became available again in the years after the war, the trays of toffee were replaced with wrapped candy which was not half so much fun for us but must have been a great deal easier for Mr. and Mrs. Dodd!

After Mr. Martin took over the shop in the late 1940's the whole ground floor was opened out into one large general store and our tiny magical hexagonal sweet store disappeared for ever.

6. Homer Damson Blossom Sunday

For a small child magic and moments of pure happiness can lie in the simplest events! Springtime for me will always be filled with memories of blossoming fruit trees everywhere, but the most anticipated was Homer Damson Blossom!

It was usually around Easter time that the news spread around the town, "Homer Damson Blossom is at its best this weekend!".

Homer, a small hamlet a couple of miles outside the town, consisted in those days of a collection of cottages and small holdings with each tenant keeping a garden and orchard, and often a couple of small fields for grazing a cow for milk and butter.

Tiny farmyards housed a pigpen or two and a few chickens for eggs and meat. Sheep with their young lambs roamed the orchards and the marginal land along the steep fields below the wooded ridge of Wenlock Edge.

At some point back in the annals of time the whole area had been planted with damson trees. They dominated every orchard, lined the laneways, and marched along every hedgerow.

How many of these trees could trace their ancestry back to the days of the Romans when Homer lay only a short distance from Viriconium, the largest Roman City in Britain. Remains of Roman Villas have been found around the area and even the name 'Homer' seems redolent of the age of Roman Occupation!

Perhaps the gardens of just such a villa were planted with the first damson trees. For it was the Romans who brought damsons to Britain almost two thousand years ago.

On Damson Blossom Sunday the sun always shone from a brilliantly blue sky! As usual, our daily family afternoon walk took us to the stackyard opposite the Crescent where the hens waited noisily for supper, then on up the Farley Road to the Windmill Hill where more hens required attention.

Finally, with Chores completed, we crossed the road and headed up the old 'Cartway'. Worn down through the ages, it was sunken deeply below the surrounding fields and filled with mud ruts which set into concrete-like runnels in dry weather and became a slippery, muddy mess after rain!

At the top of the field the 'Cartway' turned left to the 'Top Ground' but our path lay ahead over the style and between a hedgerow and green shoots of Mr. Brisbourne's winter wheat. It was quite a squeeze if we happened to meet other neighbours already returning home! The biggest sin was to tread on the wheat, far better risk hedgerow brambles every time!

A second style led us to a path winding downward though woodland which clothed the Ridge of Wenlock Edge itself. Wild garlic grew thickly here and filled the air with its own unique pungent aroma. Back then garlic was considered very foreign and I knew of no one who used it in cooking!

The last style took us out into the sunshine where Homer stretched out below us, a shimmering mass of brilliant white! Tiny thatched and tiled cottages and cow byres barely peeked through the magical foaming, sparkling sea.

Even today, 70 years later, if I shut my eyes, I am once more precariously balanced on the top step of the style, drinking in the splendour of the scene below. Alas, all too soon it would fade away, to remain just a memory, until Spring once more returned to bless our land.

When Houseman wrote

'Loveliest of trees the cherry now

Is spread with blossom along the bough

And lies about the woodland ride

Wearing white for Eastertide'

Was he really thinking of damson blossom?

,

7. The Circus Comes to Town

The arrival of the Circus was one of the highpoints of our Summer! Rumours as to the possible date circulated among us kids for weeks before at long last somebody spied the colourful notice tacked up on the Town Noticeboard outside the Town Crier's cottage! Within a half hour, it seemed almost everyone knew all about it!

That same evening Enoch Langford, resplendent in his full uniform and ringing his great bell at each stopping point, circled the town as he proclaimed.

"O Yeh! Oh Yeh! Oh Yeh! The circus is coming to town this week and will be performing their magnificent spectacle under the Big Top on Friday night Saturday afternoon and Saturday evening!"

Those approaching circus performances consumed our thoughts and conversations throughout the entire week! The thrills began on Monday or Tuesday when the circus paraded through the town to their site at the corner of Barrow Street opposite the Gasworks.

If we were lucky it was a school holiday, or their arrival was later in the day! Alas, sometimes we missed the Parade and then our only recourse was gawking over the closed Circus field gate every evening!

To have the chance to watch the parade itself was a tremendous thrill!

A stunningly beautiful lady bedecked in sequined satin and performing tricks as she 'rode' a magnificent white horse, led the Parade. She was followed by a large Calliope complete with a monkey blaring a mixture of music and advertising for the upcoming shows. Clowns of all shapes and sizes danced their way among the circus folk and onlookers handing out invitations to everyone they could reach!

A cage of monkeys chattered and bounced along. The lions in their travelling cage could be heard long before they came into view and, at least one year, there was a tiger!

Elaborate costumes bedecked the large troupe of horses and their riders. The Trapeze Artists turned cartwheels and standing somersaults along the way! The performing dogs walked on two legs and played leapfrog around their master! They were as different from our working farm dogs as chalk from cheese!

Jugglers and other solo performers filled any gaps between the wagons and finally, the ponderous, yet amazingly soft footed elephants marked the end of the Parade. Every year there were at least three elephants and occasionally a baby elephant would be tagging along. Their handler rode atop the leading beast seated gracefully behind those huge ears. How we hoped we would see him dismount for this was achieved by the elephant gracefully wrapping his trunk around his rider's waist and lowering him to the ground.

Ignoring the plethora of horse drawn waggons and lorries containing the circus folk's homes and equipment which trailed behind, we tagged along behind the elephants all the way to the gasworks field. There, Sergeant Dodd stopped us at the gate! Until we returned to see the show we could only watch from afar!

That first evening there was not much real action for the circus folk were busy setting up their homes and settling the animals for the week.

During the following days, it was quite different! If we were extraordinarily lucky, we would be hanging over the gate at precisely that wonderful moment when the Big Top Tent was raised! It was magical to watch those huge elephants walking slowly backwards as they hauled up 'The Big Top'! Performers frequently practised their acts beside their waggons and of course, the animals had to be exercised and fed!

Saturday afternoon arrived at last and we all queued with our sixpences, hoping to get 'the best seat in the house'. Some kids wanted to be in the front row! I liked to be further back on the tiered seating, high enough to see everything, too far back to be pressured into joining in any of the acts!

The seating was merely tiered mostly backless benches, sets of which formed a horseshoe shape around the show ring with the large flamboyant Performer Entrance and the Calliope completing the circle.

The tent itself seemed huge and alive with colour and music. In its centre, the show ring was enclosed with brightly painted boards about 2 ½ feet high and its floor covered with sawdust. High above stretched the high wire act ropes and swing.

Suddenly the lights dimmed, a booming fanfare rang out and the show had begun! A kaleidoscope of colour, tricks and raucous music tumbled before our enchanted eyes. We saw jugglers, tumblers, performing dogs and horses follow each other with such rapidity that they seemed but a flash in time. The high wire acts were incredible, the elephants so clever and the miniature ponies delightful to watch as they tiptoed delicately about the ring.

The biggest thrill of all came near the end when the lions in their large show cage appeared. The 'Lion-Tamer', (that's what we called him) cracked his whip as he walked among those great beasts. On command, they sat on stools, jumped over one another, rolled over and even allowed the Lion Tamer to put his head in their great jaws.

All too soon our circus was over for another year, but those wonderful memories remained with us and with time probably grew far beyond the reality of what we had really seen!

Were our circuses spectacular? We thought so. Certainly, they were our only chance to see lions, tigers, monkeys, and elephants! In those days before television, Internet, and quality colour animal magazines, the 'Just So Stories' illustrations or small black and white drawings or prints often represented our total exotic animal knowledge.

The travelling circuses gave us country children a wider perception of the world beyond our shores, and a glimpse of a vastly different lifestyle.

8. Those Lazy Summer Days

Wenlock did not have a community Swimming pool when I was young. Cooling off in hot weather required ingenuity! By the time our longed-for annual trips to the seaside arrived after the harvest in mid-September, the weather had frequently turned cool and windy! Such a minor inconvenience never stopped us. We were 'at the seaside' and we 'swam' in the waves with great enthusiasm whatever the temperature!

Before the war, we occasionally visited the Carding Mill Valley in Church Stretton on sunny Sunday afternoons. The Carding Mill Valley is a deep cleft carved by quite a small stream, into the long ridge known as the Longmynd. When the Carding Mills were operating several millponds had been created. The pond at the valley fork was popular with swimmers but considered dangerous for small children as it was quite deep. At some point post-war it was drained and the area re-naturalised.

We always stopped further down the valley and spent the afternoon playing in the shallow stream. We loved to build dams to make a paddling pool. Often Dad took us over the stream to climb a little way up the hillside where there were wimberries to be found among the patches of heather. Wimberries are sometimes called bilberries and are like blueberries but slightly

smaller.

The Cardingmill Valley, Church Stretton

Our parking place was fairly near the café where Dad used to go to buy a tray of tea. This was served from an outside window and there was always quite a queue! The hefty tray contained a big brown teapot, a jug of hot water, another of milk, a small dish of sugar and cups and saucers for all of us! It was quite a load! After our tea, it was time to return home. Since we were farmers, although the cowman might fetch the cows in and start the milking, we still had to be home in time for Dad and Mum to help in the dairy etc. and see to the other livestock.

On our last visit as a family, a week or two before war was declared, as we travelled home, Dad said "If there is a war, this is the last time we will be doing this for a very long time!"

When we were still living at the Brook House, very occasionally, on extremely hot days, we were allowed to flood the back kitchen. The latter had a concrete floor which was sloped away from the house and the back door to a low point around the off-centre drain. The back door was up two steps so a 'natural' paddling pool could be created.

Some areas were as much as five inches deep and merited an old low kitchen chair strategically placed to provide a 'diving board'! Of course, we could only jump in and the landing was hard, but a fertile imagination can work wonders from such inauspicious circumstances! Sadly, no friends were allowed!

As a special treat, we went on a picnic to Sandy Beach. This beach is located on one of the huge 'S' bends created by the River Severn as it winds across the river flats near Leighton. Mum parked our big old Vauxhall car on the roadside of the Buildwas to Shrewsbury road at approximately the nearest point and we set out across the flat grassy fields for what seemed an enormous distance before arriving at 'the beach.'

There we could paddle about on the river's edge and build castles on the tiny sand beach. It was usually extremely quiet with only another couple of families already there. We were only allowed to paddle on the very edge of the river as apparently one of the adult visitors had ventured too far and drowned! None of us had swimsuits, we just tucked our dresses into our knickers!

Mr. Haddon, Barclays' Bank Manager, lived with his wife and family of five girls at Whitwell. The previous owner had built a large oblong pool for his tropical fish collection. This pool was fed from the stream coming from Whitwell spring.

Cleaned and painted white, it became an attractive swimming pool. The one end was deep enough to allow a diving board which was mainly used for jumping in! I seem to remember that this had to be removed at some point when it was discovered that frequent jumpers were causing the floor of the pool to crack! Since the stream was spring fed, the water was extremely cold! Generally, the pool was filled and allowed to warm in the sun for a couple of weeks before it was warm enough for even the hardiest amongst us! Needless to say, every 'topping up' reduced the temperature and increased our post swim shivers dramatically!

The Haddon's were generous with their invitations and put up with the mess we must have created as we rushed into the house to dry off and warm up, with great good humour. Mr. Clark from Wigwig taught me to float on my back in Haddon's pool though I did not learn to swim until I was much older. Alas, however cold we were from our swim we soon became as hot and sticky as ever after the struggle to push our bicycles back up the steep and twisty Sheinton Bank!

Everyone counted down the days to the Annual Sunday School Trip to Rhyl! We travelled by coach and lots of the mothers came along too. Although of course we had our picnic on the beach and played in the water, my main memories of those trips are of the time we spent at Marineland funfair and of the way we sang all the way home with entertainment in the aisle provided by some of the mothers! 'Knees up Mother Brown' was a favourite!

Mother took us to Rhyl for a week's holiday towards the end of September when the harvest was finished. We stayed in a Boarding House not far from the Station. Our landlady, Mrs. Jones, cooked all our meals but Mum had to provide the food. One shelf in the sideboard was reserved for our family. Here was stored the cold roast partridge, our 'rations' and some pies and cakes which Mum had made to bring with us. Mum told Mrs. Jones what we would have to eat each meal and gave her the money to buy staples like milk, bread, and potatoes. We only had one hot meal at midday, supper was usually bread and jam and cake, and breakfast was porridge and toast.

No Matter how cold it was we spent most of the day at the beach. With Mum tucked into her rented deckchair and immersed in her novel, we were free to build castles, gather shells, and paddle as much as we wished.

At Rhyl, the sea retreats an enormous distance at low tide. When the tide is coming in it swirls around any higher sandbanks so that it is easy for young children to find themselves trapped by channels of water too deep to wade back to shore! The lifeguards, (they were dressed like policemen), rode large horses up and down the beach to make sure no one became trapped. Only once was I ignominiously slung over the saddle and carried back to the beach. Mum was so embarrassed, I felt like a criminal! Amazingly it was only years later It dawned on me that the gruff old lifeguard had in-fact saved me from at least a terrifying experience and quite likely a watery grave.

On a lighter note, we had 'swimming' lessons as part of Gym at

High School. Since we had no pool, we learned the various strokes whilst balancing our midriffs across the wooden exercise benches! The latter were about ten feet long and eight inches wide and normally used for side to side jumps or, when reversed, as balance beams. Practicing the breaststroke across that hard wooden bench was a most painful process! But at least I had some theory to guide me when I taught myself to swim as an adult and still prefer the old breaststroke or side stroke we learned! I suppose no knowledge, however limited, is ever really wasted!

Although opportunities for water play were minimal, the thrills and delight we experienced on any such occasion were multiplied precisely because of their rarity! Those special days still shine in my memory just as brightly as any of the many stunning or fantastic events which have filled my life since those early days in Wenlock!

.

9.Joe's Ride of a Lifetime!

Joe Lloyd was our town milkman. He lived in a beautiful old stone, rose draped farmhouse which lay at right angles to the Shrewsbury road at the end of a steep driveway. When Southfield Road was built in the 1920's a high retaining wall was needed to support Joe's driveway and front yard and the lovely herbaceous border which encircled it. Beyond the house the large farmgate, (seemingly always closed) effectively segregated the farmyard and buildings from the pristine 'Gentleman's Residence' which met the public eye!

Like all dairy farmers Joe and his cowman (who 'lived in') had been up before 5am for the morning milking. By 7am the housekeeper had the porridge, bacon, fried egg, crispy fried bread, and toast ready on the kitchen table. The men ate quickly and washed down their meal with large cups of strong tea before hurrying out to harness the horse and cart and load the milk.

Precisely at 7.40 am (according to Joe's old chest watch), the cowman flung back the gate and Joe drove out the great grey shire horse and loaded milk cart. The harness attested to years of 'elbow grease' as every horse brass and buckle sparkled in the early morning sun. The old high wheeled wooden milk cart had seen many decades of service, but it too glowed with cleanliness. Iron tyres clattered and milk churns clanked as the whole equipage moved steadily down the steep driveway.

The large ten-gallon milk churns were securely wedged at the front of the cart surrounded by boxes containing pint and quart milk pails and the galvanised bucket which held the dippers or ladles. He did not sell bottled milk. The pails were for sale to customers if they needed a new one. Each customer provided their own washed pail or jug into which Joe measured the requested amount of milk.

The small 'back door' of the cart was centred in a low wooden wall. It was always latched open with Joe himself standing astride in the doorway and holding the reins quite loosely as he issued intense verbal commands to his horse in the old Shropshire dialect.

This position enabled him to jump in and out quickly to serve his customers. Some customers would come out to meet him; others would leave their clean pail beside the door to be refilled. Well thumbed records of each purchase were recorded in a small notebook and most people paid up every Saturday. For many customers, this was accomplished by leaving the amount owed in the empty pail. Others enjoyed coming out to meet Joe, relishing the opportunity to catch up on village gossip.

The rattle and creak of Joe's progress around the town was so routine that folks timed their own plans by his progress. Those catching the 8am bus to Shrewsbury decided whether they had time to go to the 'terminal' and perhaps be lucky enough to get a seat or whether to run for the last stop in town with the probability of having to stand the whole 12 miles. School children planned their progress to avoid the certainty of chastisement should they not be in the school yard when the line up whistle blew.

The rhythm of morning sounds in those days was vastly different to today. There were almost no cars around and only the occasional delivery van. Petrol was rationed from 1939 to 1952. From 1942 to 1946 petrol no petrol coupons were issued for private use. This meant the streets of our small town were virtually empty of motorised vehicles. Pedestrians and cyclists had the road to themselves most of the time. Back then the clatter of hobnailed boots and cleated shoes and voices travelled the length of the street.

The strident sound of the 8.30am train whistle as it crossed over Stretton Westwood lane followed by its predictable rattle along the edge of town to the station caused any tardy Grammar School student to take off running with their heavy leather satchel bumping against their hip.

Bellows of outrage issued from any farmyard where an unhappy beast was being loaded for market. Milk churns clanked as they were lined up at the farmgate ready for pickup by the Coop lorry.

No one ever knew what alien sound spooked Joe's horse one somnolent morning. Joe himself always swore some little 'divil' with a catapult had done the deed. Certainly, one minute the old horse was plodding quietly past the High Causeway, the next, Joe's roars of outrage could be heard across town as the staid old beast reared up in the shafts and took off at a gallop.

Joe. no longer a young man, leaned precariously from the back of the cart as he threw all his weight onto the reins in an attempt to halt their flight. Smaller empty milk pails skittered backwards and launched themselves towards the road. The larger milk churns shuddered and juddered as they splashed some of their contents around them with joyous abandon! A stream of vitriolic cursing and swearing from Joe contributed to the almighty cacophony of sound.

Eventually the old horse ran out of steam and slowly drew to a standstill. It stood head drooping and sides heaving, a dejected shadow of its former self! One onlooker ran to hold the bridle. Another rushed to help Joe climb down and sit for a while on the back step to regain his breath. Within seconds the nearest housewife rushed out with our universal cure for all occasions, a nice hot cup of sweet tea!

The whole episode created a huge sensation, and the story grew ever wilder as it passed from lip to lip. Joe himself, would only give a half laugh and curse the horse should anyone inquire. Further discussion was unavailable!!!

Joe was to achieve fame of a different kind in 1949 when he was asked to be tutor for the Shropshire dialect to the cast of Gone to earth. Unfortunately, it was decided that his Shropshire was so authentic, no one would understand a word and eventually Thomas Blakemore undertook the job instead.

10. Memorable Characters of My Childhood

In childhood, we perceive the world in our own unique way. Being both short in stature and possessing unique priorities our entire perspective is distinctly different to that of the adults about us.

Growing up in the 30's and 40's in Wenlock the old axiom that children should be seen and not heard was still extraordinarily strong. In my family, I was always aware that any misbehaviour on my part would greatly embarrass my mother and my entire extended adult family in front of their friends and acquaintances. Furthermore, our Aunt Gene was fond of issuing dire warnings such as

"Don't you grow up wild like those dreadful--------- They are an absolute disgrace to the family! How their poor dear mother must have suffered from their disgraceful antics!"

Possibly, since I was the youngest and therefore most impressionable when such lectures were delivered, I learned to keep to myself my observations about the noticeably different inclinations of some of our community. We certainly had some real characters about the village who followed their own drummer to their heart's content.

Mr. Cartwright

Mr. Cartwright was one such gentleman. As was common back then, very few single men had their own house. It was far more common to rent a room in a Boarding House. Their landlady was frequently a widow for whom taking 'paying guests' was the only source of income. Lodgers rented only a room, but Boarders also had their meals provided.

Mr. Cartwright was very tall and thin. A retired Bank manager, he seemed to board in the house beyond the Stork Inn and its yard entrance. Promptly every morning he emerged impeccably turned out in full riding gear and strode into the Stork Yard where he rented a stable for his magnificent hunter.

A short while later he would ride out briskly from the Stork Yard and turn along one of the roads leading out of the town. An imposing figure, he sat bolt upright and I never saw him stop to speak to anyone or even call out a greeting! A stately nod and touch of the cap seemed the ultimate acknowledgement.

As I grew older and began to wander further afield, I frequently discovered Mr. Cartwright securely established on some wider grassy verge, with his horse, hobbled and happily grazing, nearby. He himself reclined contentedly on an old horse blanket arranged comfortably against a nearby hedgerow. Often, he appeared to be snoozing, frequently his face was hidden behind his newspaper.

Always, he was unsociable to the point of not even acknowledging my intrusion into his chosen territory. I suppose his landlady provided a packed lunch as he rarely returned home before mid to late afternoon. His routine appeared set regardless of the weather though he did return earlier on days of driving rain and did not ride out on Sundays. The only exception was his faithful attendance at every Wheatland Hunt Meet.

Every Sunday he attended the 11am service at Wenlock Church and sat alone in about the fourth or fifth row back below the pulpit. His long arms removed the need for reading glasses as he spoke and sang very loudly from a hymn or prayer book held as far out in front of his face as his arm could reach.

Little did he know that across the aisle behind him a small girl was fascinated with his every move! Long boring sermons which necessitated my sitting very quietly without fidgeting were a wonderful time for dreaming and imagining lives and stories about other worshippers! Mr. Cartwright played the hero or villain in many of my imaginings!

Snifty

Snifty_was our local tramp, I don't know his real name. I believe he suffered from what would nowadays be called PTSD because of his experiences in WW1. He wandered around the district, making his home each night in one of the many wooded areas. Occasionally he provided casual labour to needy farmers. Naturally, we children were all distrustful of someone who dared to be so different and some of the boys would make taunting derisive remarks in his hearing. Snifty would respond with a yell and wave his stick, otherwise we had little contact.

One summer's day I was invited to visit my friend at her farm in Bourton and we spent the day playing about the village and neighbouring coppices. Hide and Seek was a favourite game. Rushing to find a hiding place before my friend counted to one hundred, I sped towards the massive trunk of an ancient horse chestnut tree. With no time to spare I dived behind only to almost land on top of Snifty in his small campsite. I don't know who was more surprised! He yelled and I screamed and ran! My terror was infectious and we both ran screaming back to the farmhouse kitchen!

Placated with milk and a jam-butty, (our name for a thick slice of bread spread with either margarine or jam), we soon calmed down, although the older members of the family had a good laugh at our expense!

The experience did not stop my love of wandering all about the countryside, but I did learn to be more cautious and pay more attention to my immediate surroundings! Had I been observant I could easily have smelt the smoke from his small fire and possibly even seen it wafting out from behind the tree!

Our Roadmen

Nowadays, roadside hedgerows are trimmed mechanically, and road sweepers make short work of any mess. Back then, none of the roads or lanes around of Wenlock were curbed, and all were lined with ancient hedgerows. Over the centuries, the roads had gradually sunk down so that the hedges themselves sat atop grassy banks.

Many farmworkers became 'roadmen' when they neared retirement. Heading out of town to their allotted section each morning armed with a wheelbarrow, a scythe, shears, and a shovel, they often had quite a long walk of several miles! The system seemed to work well for the most part although during the peak growing season the hedge bank growth in the as yet untended stretches did creep into the road space considerably.

Fortunately, the weight of traffic in those days was so light that this presented only a minor inconvenience. Of course, Mr. Cartwright's horse and the occasional tethered goat did help keep down the flatter verges quite efficiently!

During my last year at Coalbrookdale Grammar School I developed a tendency to excruciating migraines. Quite unable to function I was given permission to go home. I suppose I could have caught the Noon train but discovered that walking back up to Wenlock invariably cured my migraine and I could settle down to study at home. Traffic even in 1953 was light, farm vehicles and the occasional delivery truck providing the bulk of the mid-morning traffic.

Frequently the only person I encountered and passed the time of day with was the roadman working the Farley Dingle stretch. A soft spoken and gentle elderly man, his knowledge of nature and obvious contentment with his daily grind were very therapeutic at a time when the pressure to do well in my upcoming exams was overwhelming! Our conversations taught me that nothing is more important than appreciating the world we have. Happiness is all about enjoying what we have, not having what we think we want!

The Gypsies

The gypsies generally arrived in town in Spring or Autumn. We would see their Romany caravans making their way toward the Callaughton road where they often camped. The men often worked as casual labourers on one of the local farms, the women sold pegs and ribbons door to door around the town usually with a clutch of small children at their heels. Within a day or two of their arrival the Truant Officer would round up the older children to attend school. It must have been purgatory facing both the suspicion of the other children and the teachers' obvious irritation and annoyance at the disruption caused by their arrival.

If the gypsy menfolk found casual work during the week, they patronised the local Pubs with enthusiasm come Saturday night! The result was arrest and a night in Jail for being drunk and disorderly!

Within an hour of their internment, a large cohort of gipsy wives and mothers set up camp on the pavement in front of the Police Station, (and opposite my bedroom window,) where they seemed to set up a continuous wailing and crying until the men were released next morning. In truth, I do not know how many women continued their vigil throughout the night, but they were certainly there on mass to greet the prisoners when released the next morning! The miscreants were escorted back to the gipsy camp like conquering heroes!

In a few short weeks, the gypsies would move on once more and life would settle back into the seasonal patterns established by our ancestors throughout the ages!

Mrs. Evans

My mother worked part-time on the farm as well as looking after us children and the house. She looked after the dairy and our large flock of chickens. After my father's death in 1942, she was forced to become a full-time farmer too! Prior to the war, we had had a maid who usually lived in and started working for us as soon as she left school. I suppose today she would be called a 'Mothers' Helper'!

Once the war started all the young people went to work in the munition factory in Ditton Priors and Mum was very happy when Mrs. Evans agreed to 'do' for us 3 mornings a week. She ran a tight ship! We children all learned that Mrs. Evans word was law, no excuses were tolerated!

Our ancient black oak front door with its beautiful stained-glass window was only just over 5 feet high. The floor of our old house had sunk over the centuries and it was a big step down for small girls to the red tiled hall floor.

On Fridays, when Susan and I came clattering in at lunch time, a trail of newspapers led across the sparkling tiles to where Mrs. Evans, was on her knees busy with scrubbing brush and floor cloth.

"Don't you kids tread on my clean floor or you're for it!" she yelled. "Look at the state of your shoes! Stay on the papers and don't shuffle them around!

Mum hated anyone calling us kids but no matter what Mrs. Evans chose to call us, her word was law!

Obediently we tiptoed along the paper trail, stepping carefully on each page of yesterday's News and through the door which led to the back hall and the coat racks. Beneath them a cloth and a knife stood ready. Dutifully, we scraped and wiped our offending shoes to Mrs. Evans' satisfaction before running through the scullery to the kitchen. We wore our shoes inside and out in those days. Slippers were reserved for bedtime routines.

I learned another side of Mrs. Evans when I became extremely ill for several weeks. She proved to be the kindest gentlest nurse possible and I loved to see her come into the bedroom always with a smile and a joke! When we moved up to Arlescott she continued to 'do for us', riding the bus up from Wenlock two or three times a week and managing in appallingly primitive conditions to do our laundry and clean our rooms. By this time Mum was back teaching full time and life would have been even more difficult without our loyal friend and helper, Mrs. Evans!

11. Grandad's Glorious Gardens

We British have always loved our gardens! Blest with rainfall which can best be described as little and often, gardening provides rich rewards for even the casual gardener!

When Grandad Yates was a boy the George Inn garden had long been turned into a cider making yard. His youthful memories consisted of helping to plant the Linden Avenue and his love of the beautiful gardens surrounding the Abbey which he would visit during the annual Church fete held on the Priory lawn. His Aunty Alice Ainsworth's garden at the Brook House Farm may have provided both his inspiration and practical education.

Thomas and Alice Ainsworth had created both a working and pleasure garden with so much love that eighty years later, that old garden still carried its ethereal timelessness in our very uncertain world! Wandering its paths gave me immense pleasure, virtually imparting a spiritual renaissance, one that truly delivered balm for the soul.

When Grandad moved his own young family to the Brook House Farm in the mid 1890's he inherited and continued to improve this wonderful old walled garden. Grandma delighted in gathering enormous armfuls of blooms to fill every corner of the old farmhouse and later The George Inn, and Grandad was happy to have a reason to provide them!

The small 'summer house' consisted of a railway carriage, (minus wheels), so venerable that its design was nearer that of a stagecoach than a modern passenger coach. Entry was through double doors, (I suppose these were required to accommodate the hoop skirts so fashionable during the Victorian era), flanked with small windows. The bench seats either side each held two, possibly three people. The old, curved roof was reinforced with corrugated iron sheets and the windows and doors on the 'back' were panelled over.

Two steps down led to a small patio surrounded with latticed arches which carried a profusion of red roses in season. It was under one of these arches that my sister and I buried all our dolls in a solemn funeral after my father's death.

The central path, (all the pathways seemed wide enough for a crinoline gown to move with ease), led to a large stone fishpond, the centre of the garden and the meeting point of the four pathways which quartered the whole design.

The high rear wall was hidden from view by an enormous wooden scaffolding which was always smothered in thick leafy loganberry vines. The loganberry 'wall' was set forward of the old brick wall to allow picking from both sides. The centre entrance was often completely arched over with vines and presented a frightening 'black hole' to small girls! For many years, I thought that Adam and Eve must have hidden beyond that sinister hole after they had eaten the forbidden apple, something that we ourselves were inclined to do on occasion!

One side of the garden was lined with fruit trees behind an irregular line of thirteen huge blackcurrant bushes and two gooseberry bushes. How can I be so precise? I learned to count to thirteen with those bushes! The ground beneath was carpeted with white and purple rock and blue, white, and pink forget-me-nots.

In early July, our focus was the small summer apple tree. Its tiny apples, scarcely bigger than a golf ball, were as sweet as sugar itself. The wasps told us when the apples were perfect. Then it became a race between us and the wasps to clear the tree. Strangely enough, those apples would not even keep a day or too. They had to be enjoyed freshly picked which suited us kids fine!

We loved to climb the gnarly old cider apple tree beside the summer house, to pull and eat thin forced rhubarb stalks, early peas and beans and raspberries and strawberries in season. I think we ate everything except the caterpillars which festooned all the cabbage family plants! In caterpillar season, we 'earned' our Saturday pennies picking pails of caterpillars for extinction! Even so, in the days before pesticides, all of our green vegetables carried 'holes' where the caterpillars had enjoyed a meal before us.

The other side wall sheltered a massive iron water tank sunk deep into the earth, an old, galvanised bath full of mint, a large bed of parsley, the compost heap and two huge horseradish plants. Every Sunday morning my father would dig up a piece of horseradish root. Roast beef without freshly grated horseradish was unthinkable for my father and mother!

Perennial flowers, particularly spring bulbs were scattered around wherever they chose to grow, and a row of sweet peas and colourful runner beans glowed among the vegetables. A huge herbaceous border flanked the old summerhouse. Here grew the peonies, Iris, poppies, white and yellow daisies, and chrysanthemums which provided the mammoth displays on the hearth in front of our pinecone filled fireplace. No one had a living room fire in summer!

Grandad's next garden was almost accidental, purely a pleasure garden! The project started out as a campout playhouse for his six young children. Around the turn of the century, he had managed to beg or buy an old railway carriage from the early days of the 'Wellington, Wenlock and Craven Arms Railway'. It was quite small, maybe fifteen feet long with two doors on each side.

On the highest point of the 'Top Ground', (the name given the field beyond the Sytche Coppice) was an ancient small shallow quarry. It was the perfect spot for the new camp playhouse! The upper end was levelled off to provide a platform for the old carriage (now minus its wheels). Its interior was gutted, then panelled and papered, and lino (linoleum) laid over the wooden floor. A corrugated iron roof and a new coat of paint completed the exterior. A flat terrace in front was wide enough to accommodate 2 or 3 deck chairs.

The interior was equipped with tables and benches, the cupboards were stocked with old iron cooking pots and frypans, cutlery, tin or enamel mugs and plates. A small paraffin stove provided cooking facilities for those occupants who brought along their own supply of paraffin! Bunk beds lined the one wall and bits of old rugs were scattered around the floor.

The whole quarry area was securely fenced against the cows that normally grazed the fields which had been grassland for centuries.

The completed camp playhouse was enormously popular with the children. Here, in the carefree years before the 1st World War, they camped out on summer nights with their friends and watched the myriad stars above the dark hillside. Even in the 1940's it was still being borrowed by the scouts and other groups either for daytime events or the occasional sleepover.

Grandad determined that he would turn the area in front of this summerhouse into a pleasure garden for his beloved wife, Kate. The newly created quarry gardens in Shrewsbury dingle were his inspiration!

With four sons to provide plenty of enthusiasm and manpower, they built a beautiful little sunken garden filled with daffodils, white and purple rock and surrounded with heaving mounds of white and purple lilac bushes.

A Sunday afternoon picnic at the Summer House became a tradition every Spring for many years. When I was a child the whole garden was suffering from benign neglect, but the lilacs still bloomed over the masses of daffodils waving above a sea of white and purple rock. My father occasionally still ran the ancient mower over the small grass patches each side the central path and we all loved to explore the summerhouse whilst Mum and Dad enjoyed the old deck chairs on the 'terrace'.

Alas, today everything is gone, only a flat field remains!

Grandad's third garden initiated the beginning of essential healing for his broken heart!

One hot Summer's day in early June 1933 Kate had dropped dead whilst removing her hat after an afternoon walk. A vibrant active woman and a keen lawn bowler, Kate was involved with every facet of Wenlock Life.

Five years younger and never ever sick, Kate was Fred's rock and his reason for living. Her death left him completely demoralized to such an extent that he completely lost all desire to live! He had his own name and 'died 19' carved below her name on the gravestone. It was only with the greatest difficulty that his children prevented him having '193'! Eventually they had to ask the stonemason to just leave off the 3 'in error'!

The necessity to continue working with his sons in the family businesses kept him functioning throughout that first winter. But when Spring arrived his passion for gardens resurfaced and he determined to make a garden almost opposite the cemetery as a living tribute to his darling Kate.

He rented the triangle of land between the Bridgnorth and Callaughton roads and fashioned an iron garden gate with Evan Evans, the Blacksmith's help, for the narrow entrance at the meeting point of the two roads. With a family history of blacksmithing Fred had spent time in his Uncle William Yates' Blacksmith shop on the Shrewsbury road when in his youth and Evan had taken over the business when William retired.

A centre path divided the triangle of land equally and each year the garden grew larger. The first few yards were filled with blackcurrant, red currant, and gooseberry bushes, then came the mandatory rows of vegetables and of course the strawberry rows travelled along the vegetable patches year by year. There were always six rows; two newly planted, two second year which produced good berries but did not carry a large crop and two third year rows that produced in abundance.

Yet another old train carriage was located and set up overlooking his emerging flower garden. Entrance to this area was under huge arches of climbing yellow, white, and red roses. The flower garden itself had small paths running in all directions with everything leading to the center castles and stone 'lake'. The latter was an old oval stone sink placed strategically between two large rocks each of which was topped with a castle of gleaming white round towers with steep pointed red roofs.

Grandad had made the castles himself by pouring concrete into tin cans and cones of assorted sizes. Doors, windows, a draw bridge, and docks at the water's edge completed the fantasy.

An orchard and a myriad of garden sheds multiplied beyond, but for we children the magic of the garden lay with the summerhouse, the intricate winding pathways among the flowers and the castles and Grandad's stories!

Almost every Saturday morning during the summer months we would walk with Grandad to his garden. His daily routine never changed; a large bowl of porridge and apple sauce for breakfast with lots of tea (he had only one tooth and refused to try false teeth), a short rest beside the back door then at 9.30am it was time to head to his garden.

Walking together up to the garden was fun! Grandad would tell us stories about Wenlock when he was young, the Morrell ancestor who died at the battle for Bridgnorth castle, Plum Pudding Hill built overnight by the Roundheads before that battle, Major Smallman from Wilderhope who jumped his horse over Wenlock Edge to escape the Roundheads and old legends like the giant making the Wrekin.

Grandad never ever spoke of his wife or his own family! In fact, I did not know that the old man living beside us at the Brookhouse was his brother until years after they were both dead!

Our arrival at the garden seemed almost a ritual! The large padlock on the gate needed an equally large key and was opened with great ceremony! A similar lock secured the old railway carriage which Grandad had turned into his own cozy living room. A mantel shelf over the mock fireplace carried two large Doulton dancing ladies their magnificent blue and pink skirts held high above their heads. They flanked a small biscuit barrel which often contained a few treats, probably bought with Grandad's own

Sweet ration! Murals adorned the cream painted walls; I remember particularly the large 'WEN' inside an equally large old-fashioned lock and several dancing figures. A couple of old settles and Grandad's wooden armchair provided seating.

1938 or 9. Grandad sits beside his completed castles!

After a short rest, we would all walk about the small flower garden admiring and learning the names of the various flowers and bushes before finally arriving at the castles in the centre! Here we entered a fantastic world of princesses, dragons, wicked witches, every variety of fairy folk and, naturally, ogres of every description! With tiny figurines for us to play out the story, we discovered a magical kingdom where Grandad reigned supreme!

Alas, all to soon, it was time to start home. The ritual of locking up completed we walked across the road to the cemetery to visit Granny's grave and stare at that inscription with our beloved Grandad's name 'Died 19 '. There were other stops to be made, Uncle Jamie who had died in the war, our own father, Grandad's son Donald and Cousin Thomas Joseph who was a 'great respected teacher'. He had taught at Onibury his entire career, was headmaster when he retired. Thomas Joseph never married. Grandad admired his cousin as a great scholar and very learned man!

It was a sombre little group that meandered home down racecourse lane between the high banked hedgerows. At that time Hodgecroft and Swan Meadow were still open fields and we generally walked in a wide line that spread across the entire road. In the unlikely event of any traffic, we would have heard it coming long before it reached us. The little Tollgate House and the high walls surrounding the Burt family mansion marked the junction with St Mary's Lane as once again we said Goodbye to Grandad at the back door to the George and returned to reality!

The picture below was taken in 1958 the year after Mr. Yates' death. The castles became more enchanted as the garden around flourished!

12. Camping With The Guides

The end of the war brought an intense desire to return to normal recreational activities. Both the Guides and Scouts were anxious to resume their camping trips to the seaside. The first Post-War Guide trip was a memorable experience for me.

Miss B. had booked a camping field for one week at Llangwynadl on the Lleyn Peninsula in Wales and managed to rent sufficient x-army Bell tents plus a larger community tent to house the two dozen or so girls who signed up for the great adventure.

Unfortunately, she was not having so much luck in finding a qualified Guider who would be responsible for the organisation of meals and the cooking. Eventually, my mother, who had belonged to the guides throughout Grammar School and run her own Guide Troupe for several years before her marriage, agreed to the job. My sister had joined the guides the previous year, but I was still too young. However, it was agreed that Mum could take me as her 'helper'. I would join in the general activities but stay with my mother and help in the cookhouse most of the time.

Bursting with excitement, we caught the 8.30 am train one sunny August morning, each with our pack of sandwiches squished into a mackintosh pocket, a small suitcase and kitbag of bedding. The chances of being able to buy food as we changed trains were slim and most of us had very little money anyway. Even the leaders had their sandwiches and vacuum flasks of tea. Water fountains or bathroom tap water would suffice for the rest of us.

The journey required several changes and, as always in those days, the trains were absolutely packed. Much of the journey was spent sitting on our luggage in the corridors or waiting on crowded platforms for connecting trains. By the time we arrived at Pwllheli on the Llyn Peninsula it was already late afternoon. The thrill of our arrival was dampened somewhat by the weather, which was cold, windy and wet.

We crowded into the small Ladies Waiting Room to wait, it seemed for ever, for Miss B to contact our pre-arranged transport which would take us to our farm campsite. The latter was some 12 or 13 miles from Pwllheli. We had had quite a long singsong before she finally returned with our driver who helped carry out some of the larger group supplies for us. We were to travel in an x-army lorry. The Guides packed into the back like sardines, using their luggage as seats once more, and the driver tied down the canvas back flap to 'keep them warm and dry'! I sat on my mother's lap beside the driver and Miss B. squeezed in beside us!

Twelve miles is a long way when the whole distance is travelled on poorly maintained narrow country lanes. Luckily for us, there was little other traffic. The couple of vehicles we did meet required our driver backing to the nearest wider grass edge and bumping up to hang, (to a chorus of squeals from the back) at what seemed a crazy angle for few seconds before bouncing down again and continuing on our way.

The further north we travelled the wetter and windier it seemed to get. At last, we pulled into a cobbled farmyard. It was blowing a gale and the slanting rain drove sideways in great sheets. Our tents had been delivered and were stored in the barn, but it was obviously impossible to erect those heavy canvas bell tents that night!

Wearily we climbed out and huddled in the shelter of the barn whilst Miss B and my mother went into the farmhouse to discuss the situation. The farmer and his wife were elderly and unused to much company. But they were, above all, kind and welcoming. Faced with a bedraggled group of cold and hungry kids they really turned up trumps. Stoking up the fire in the big black kitchen range the old farmer helped Mum get a large pot of milk set to heat. The patrol leaders were sent to the barn to find our enamel bowls and spoons. Soon we were all enjoying a large (and very welcome) bowl of bread and milk.

It was decided that we would all have to sleep on the floor in the living room and kitchen that night, and to that end, furniture was moved out or stacked to free up sufficient floor space. A similar process in their small spare bedroom accommodated some of the older girls and the Leaders. Because I was so small and sickly, the farmer's wife decided I needed more coddling. She pushed the two armchairs face to face and lifted me and my blankets into the tiny bed this created. Within minutes I was asleep until brilliant sunshine woke us all early the next morning.

Before the leaders went to bed, they had dug out a large cooking pot and set the porridge to cook overnight on the old kitchen range. By the time we had all visited the outhouse, washed under the pump, and repacked our bedding, our porridge was ready. To my disgust, it was salted! But there was fresh milk from the cow the farmer had hand milked that morning.

Stoked with those large bowls of porridge, we streamed out into the sunshine and Miss B. called Reveille. Then the Guides split into their Patrol Groups and started to set up camp in the big field beyond the house. Away in the distance we could just catch a tempting glimpse of the sea with the morning sun shining across the waves. It was a first for many of us and just the inspiration we needed for everyone to tackle their tasks with enthusiasm.

Soon the big bell tents and the kitchen tent were up. I 'helped' set up the long open fireplace pit and enthusiastic foraging for wood by the kitchen patrol produced enough for Mum to get a fire started. Getting enough wood was to be a constant battle since we were reliant on dead wood collected around the hedgerows although I think the farmer took pity on Mum and did provide a few dry logs from his woodpile.

The patrol digging the latrines had the hardest job! The land was rough and stony and sodden from the heavy rain. The holes were supposed to be at least 18 inches deep with a pile of soil and spade beside each hole for covering any solid matter after use. In reality, the diggers had a job to go even a foot deep! During the week the latrine walls, (vertical canvas, pegged to posts held upright with guy ropes) blew down at least twice a day!

Eight guides slept in each Bell tent. The big centre pole held hooks for our outdoor clothes and each of us had an ex-army cape which doubled as our groundsheet. None of us had sleeping bags. We had been instructed to bring two wool blankets, a sheet and a pillow. By folding the blankets and sheet top to bottom we could 'envelope' the layers into a bed which had the same thickness both above and below and just fitted (most of the time) on our groundsheet.

It was a matter of pride to the Guides that no sign of our campsite should remain when we left! This meant that nothing could lie on the grass during the day. Four wooden stakes beside each bedspace provided a perch for our suitcase. During the day, our bedding was folded and piled on our case and our groundsheets hung on the centre pole. Whatever the weather the 'skirt' of the bell tent and the door-flap was rolled up.

I think our first dinner, (we all had dinner at midday in those days) was hot tea, baked beans and bread. We had carried a sack of summer windfall apples from Wenlock and they provided desert.

Some communal supplemental rations were provided for group activities and these had been ordered locally and were already in the barn. I remember sacks of Quaker Oats, potatoes, carrots, turnips, onions, trays of bread and big tins of custard powder and cocoa and a bag of powdered egg.

After a huge discussion about the availability of shops with a delivery service anywhere near our camp and our total lack of any transport, it had been decided that each girl would purchase and bring her own rations.

As soon as the kitchen patrol had completed their cleanup duties the girls were sent to fetch these 'rations' from their suitcase. Poor Mum! As each girl stepped up to the table to deposit their tiny squishy smelly packages of sugar, cheese, margarine, and bacon the resulting pile appeared to be nothing short of a disaster!

Miss B.'s shrill whistle created a headlong rush to assemble at the flagpole. A busy afternoon was planned for the girls. They would be working on their various badges with games to follow.

Mum squeezed an extra cuppa of evil looking tea from the blackened kettle and sat down by the dismal fire with me on her knee. A short rest before we tackled those evil smelly packages!

"I think I must be getting a cold" she murmured sniffling a bit, but I was not fooled!

Those few tears were all she allowed herself before we set to work.

We started on the bacon first! Mum set a large pan of water over the fire and added enough wood to bring it to a boil.

My job was to unwrap each package – the bacon ration was about three slices per person per week – and flatten each slice. Many slices and packs contained white greasy bacon worms who were busily eating the precious bacon.

Mum scraped the worms from each side of each slice and piled the cleaned slices on a plate. When the water boiled, she added the bacon pile and kept it boiling for five minutes. The despised worms and packaging became extra fuel and our fire sizzled and spit with enthusiasm.

The only means of draining and drying the strips was a wire mesh cooling tray, but it was quite efficient and soon the bacon was packed away in a covered pan, waiting to be fried for breakfast the next morning!

It actually fried up quite nicely and all the girls ate their bacon 'butties' enthusiastically. Only Mum and I knew why I had suddenly developed a dislike of bacon and a love of bread and marmite!

But back to our ration salvaging project! The margarine was easy. We just scraped it all into a big jar where it soon congealed into one large greasy blob from which it could easily be scraped and spread on bread or toast. The lard also was scraped into a big jar. Some was used for frying or cooking, a great deal became fried bread which was popular for breakfast. Sugar was only a problem when it had set into lumps from the damp but the cheese was our greatest challenge!

Once again, I unwrapped, and Mum scraped off any mold. This time she did not bother too much about the odd cheese worm. Apparently, in her childhood the large wheels of homemade cheese which lasted many weeks had often developed worms! She told me how her father had ridiculed any of the children who fussed saying,

"They grew in the cheese, all they ate was cheese, ignore them and eat up!"

This time the tiny hunks of cheese were grated and set aside for macaroni cheese which would be our dinner the next day.

Looking back, it seems to me we ate an awful lot of bread or toast with margarine or jam (it was always one or the other never both). Marmite was popular with some of the girls and small jars of fish paste provided sandwiches for our 'tea'. Tea was our name for the evening meal, usually eaten about 5pm. Midday meals were mainly potatoes and vegetables with a sausage or slice of spam or corned beef. At home, for a real treat Mum fried spam slices dipped in pancake batter. But I don't remember whether she did this on our first or second camping trip.

Somehow Mum managed to feed us all with that smoky fire burning mostly wet and living wood and putting out little heat. But, when she was asked to be cook again the following year, she made several stipulations! First, a load of good firewood had to be delivered and stacked near to the cooking area. Secondly, the 'rations' would be purchased as a special order from a nearby store and the campsite itself should be selected within walking distance of a small store. Thirdly, better kitchen equipment would be hired! The latter included decent fireplace grates, a couple of full height tables to work on and several large iron frying pans!

We did make the long trek to the beach on three afternoons and paddled and played in the waves. Few of us could swim even a few strokes and Miss B. soon called us out to dress and play beach games to 'warm up'. Most of us were shivering in the chilly wind and were happy to return to camp and a hot drink.

The weather was to remain cold and windy throughout our stay with very few sunny hours.

My favourite part of the whole holiday was when we all gathered around the campfire in the evening and sang as we drank our bedtime cocoa.

'There's a long, long snail a crawling across the top of my bed,'

'Ten green bottles hanging on the wall,'

'One man went to mow, went to mow a meadow,'

And, sung with deep feeling,

'Incey, wincey spider climbing up the spout,

Down came the rain and washed the spider out,

Out came the sun and dried up all the rain,

Incey wincey spider climbing up again!'

The evenings ended with my favourite twilight hymn:

'Days done, gone the sun, from the sea, from the hills, from the sky.

All is well, safely rest, God is nigh!

13. August Monday Celebrations

When Wenlock Annual Olympic Games resumed after WW2 August Monday became once more the most exciting day of the year! But the day included much more than just sports and was the culmination of many of our town's summer activities.

Sometime in late May or early June two 'dances' were held in the Memorial Hall. The Children's Dance was mainly a social event with lots of organised games and some entertainment. Funnily enough, I have no recollection as to whether there were any refreshments! In those far of days of rationing, we did not expect food anywhere except at our own home.

The main purpose of the event was to select the Carnival Princess and her six attendants. The judge was usually a member of the local aristocracy. Every girl who wished to compete formed a large circle around the Judge and other Officials. Endeavouring to look as pretty as possible, we smiled, walked in a circle, stood for inspection and generally held our breath in suspense, it seemed for ever!

Finally, the Judge began calling forward the chosen few. Sometimes he would choose the Carnival Princess first, other years he would choose seven girls and then select the Carnival Princess from among the seven.

One year I was chosen as an attendant and was ecstatic until I went home! My mother was furious! It transpired that I had only been allowed to enter because she was sure I was too plain and did not stand a chance of selection. She was extremely annoyed at having to use valuable clothing coupons to purchase material to make a white dress which would have to be dyed afterwards if I was to get any real use out of it!

"Lord Forester must need his eyes checking, choosing you with your straight black hair and square face. You must have smiled at just the right time; you do have a nice smile."

Confidence building was not high on parent's lists in those days, we were frequently told we would never amount to anything unless!!!! One of our Headmaster's favourite tirades included the fact that we were all such laggards we would end up making the pips for raspberry jam! During the war years, most jams contained a large amount of swede and it was a general belief that the number of pips far outweighed the number of berries and therefore must have been artificially produced!

The evening Dance was a much grander affair with all the older girls turning out in their prettiest dresses with freshly styled hair. My only knowledge of this event was limited to seeing folks walking past our windows towards the Memorial Hall. However, at some point in the evening, the Carnival Queen and her six attendants were selected.

In early June Nancy Clifford began signing up the thirty girls she needed to train for the Maypole Dancing. We practised twice a week under the Corn Exchange to the accompaniment of

Nancy's own wind-up gramophone and Nancy's voice calling 'one, two, three, HOP!'

Wind-up gramophones have a limited play time. At frequent intervals, the music would slow down and begin to groan out its dying notes. This precipitated a headlong rush from Nancy or one of the bystanders to wind up the gramophone ASAP as we endeavoured to adjust our hop to fit the changing tempo.

In and out we wove our red, yellow, blue, and green ribbons, single wrap, single weave, two over, two under, and then repeated the same patterns dancing in couples. We plaited the pole each time until we were all gathered around the base with but a yard of free ribbon left. On Nancy's brisk command we all turned around and began the careful process of unwinding our ribbons until we were tethered only to the top of the Maypole and its long green pole was completely bare. One wrong move caused a frantic "Stop!" and a rush to carefully lift the needle from the record on the gramophone.

Not only the one original mistake had to be reversed but every dancer had to go back however many moves were involved. Nancy's careful instructions usually worked but sometimes it seemed the tangle grew rather than shrank particularly towards the end of our practice hour!

The Tennis and Bowling Clubs were busy planning, practising, and finalising their teams. I believe their main competitors were other local clubs but the Athletics and Cycling events attracted regional participants.

For the older folks or those less athletically inclined there were the Flower and Vegetable competitions and the needlework, knitting and cookery competitions which were housed in two large marquees set up beside the swings. There were some cash prizes but the thrill of winning a 1st place far outweighed the value of the Prize.

I loved entering the Children's vase of wildflowers competition! My display consisted of masses of hedgerow flowers arranged in a large stoneware pot. Other favourites were 'A Garden on a Plate' and 'A Bouquet in an Egg-Cup'. One year the winning 'Bouquet in an Eggcup' consisted of an arrangement of red runner bean flowers in a blue eggcup.

The Sunday before was a hive of activity as the Queen, Princess, attendants, and their families helped to decorate their Floats. All around the town other groups were working to complete as much of their entry as possible. Horses were groomed till they shone, their leather and Brasses were polished, lorries washed, bicycles and prams cleaned and decorated. The gardeners were harvesting and polishing their fruit and vegetables; the ladies were busy baking and putting the finishing touches to needlework and I was wandering the hedgerows and coppices picking my wildflowers and chunks of moss needed to form the 'lawn' of my 'Garden on a Plate'.

The whole town was astir very early on the day itself. Many of the people rushing to the Games Ground to arrange their entries in the Horticulture and Home Craft marquees were also involved with floats and performed various official duties during the day itself!

The Carnival Parade produced packed streets with entries of decorated horse drawn drays or lorries representing every Club. There were many individual entries too. Once assembled in the Goods yard on the new Road the various classes were judged, and Rosettes awarded. before the young Herald on his pony led the Parade through the town

The big shire horses were resplendent as they bent to their task, horse brasses and harness glittered, and manes and tails were plaited with red, white and blue ribbons. In between the medley of horse drawn floats and lorries were Brass Bands, decorated bicycles, prams, and pushcarts. The main source of all our decorations was crepe paper! This could be wound through spokes, twisted into streamers, or made into rosettes. The communal effort on the Queen and Princess Drays had us all making crepe paper rosettes for days!

Either Anne or Dorothy Cookson on right, myself on left with our Carnival Princess, Mary Langford, behind.

Reaching the Square, the Queen, Princess, and their attendants climbed down and assembled in front of the clock for the official crowning of the Queen and her Court. This was completed with great formality by a prominent person, to loud cheers! Newspaper photographers documented the whole affair and anyone lucky enough to have a camera carefully chose their shots. Film and its development was a major expense back then!

Soon it was time to resume the parade! The Queen and her court climbed back aboard their floats to lead the Parade up to the Linden Playing Fields or, as we called it, the Games Ground!

The empty stage beneath the town clock proved a wonderful photo opportunity for local children as they hammed it up for cameras.

Meanwhile the area of the Games Ground near the gates which was our Soccer Pitch in winter had been turned into a huge carpark! Latecomers lined Station road and the Slang. Many of those watching the Parade followed along and went immediately onto the Grounds. Some of us detoured home for a quick lunch. Others headed back to their cars to enjoy a picnic.

There was fierce competition among the WI members in the bottled fruit, jam, Victoria Sponge and other baked goods classes. It seemed that all the ladies and most of the girls entered the knitting and embroidery classes. When the marquees were reopened at 1pm there was great excitement or consternation for many competitors! Had they won the coveted 1st place card, if not perhaps a 2nd or 3rd would be OK, but it really depended who had beaten them!

As the participants and their families wandered around the exhibits many of them, their supporters and frequently spectators were loudly or quietly critical of the Judge's choices. But such is always the case!

At the end of the day, some flower displays, garden produce, and baked goods were auctioned off, others chose to take their efforts home. But although nothing could enhance or reduce the very real satisfaction and pleasure enjoyed in the expectation and preparation, actually winning positively exhilarating!

Archery on the School Playing Field

Further along the gamesground athletic competitions were in full swing. I loved watching the bicycle races with each one trying to not to be the leader when it came to the final sprint and the Long jump and High Jump. The latter was still the standard scissor jump, but competitors reached remarkable heights.

I have only one memory of 'Climbing the Greasy Pole" and even that is of the waiting pole itself. We danced the Maypole near the Cricket Wicket Pitch which was roped off to prevent damage! One year a gymkhana filled the Cutler's Yard across the railway footbridge, another year there was an Archery competition in the School Playing Field. The highlight of a Wenlock summer, our very own Olympic games remain, even today, a much-loved memory of my teenage years.

14. Shopping Days in Shrewsbury

A busy Day on Mardol in 1958

Memories of those special red-letter days when we went into town really separate into two time periods, when we had the farm and after Mum returned to teaching!

Visits before my father's death and until we gave up the farm were always connected with the animal markets and our occasional inclusion in such trips was usually caused by the need to take us shopping for clothes or shoes or the simple fact that there would be no one at home to look after us!

Monday was Market day in Wenlock and Bridgnorth. Our local Wenlock Market was at the Smithfield Yard just beyond the Goods Station Yard and coal-wharf. Occasionally Dad would take us with him. It was fun to see all the animals in their pens and feel the air so thick with their dust and absorb the cacophony of sounds generated by several hundred animals. The smell didn't register. We lived with a manure heap not far from our backdoor which was replenished daily from the cowsheds and spread on the fields each fall or spring.

For Dad, it was a chance to chat with friends in the farming business, so we children had plenty of time to stand and stare!

One memorable trip when I was very young was to the autumn sheep markets in Welshpool. The huge crowds of people restricted my view of the world to a succession of large, studded boots. Suddenly among the feet coming towards me I saw two enormous boots. To me they looked two or three times as big as my Daddy's boots and I was very scared and started to cry. Daddy put me up onto his shoulder and told me that those feet belonged to a man who was a giant who lived in the hills. That scared me even more! I dreamed about that giant for an exceedingly long time!

Tuesday was Market day in Shrewsbury. Dad usually went to the Market in Shrewsbury and only occasionally to Bridgnorth. Often Mum went with him. In Bridgnorth she could meet up with her family and Shrewsbury was our main shopping centre. Farmers received a petrol ration for attending market.

Pride Hill, Shrewsbury in 1958. Much steeper than it looks! It was usually a crawling mass of cars cranking though the gears and the dreaded part of every mandatory driving test!

If we were extremely lucky Mum and Dad, and later just Mum, would take us to Shrewsbury on Market Day. Dad spent the morning at the livestock market where he often had an animal for sale or perhaps one he needed to buy. Bryan usually stayed with Dad and we would spend the morning shopping!

We met for dinner at one o'clock at Boots restaurant. The meal was always the same; Brown Windsor Soup (which I dislike to this day), Mashed Potatoes, usually Cabbage or Beans and Carrots, a slice of meat and Dark Brown Gravy. Everything was brought to the table in covered silver dishes from which the adults served themselves and Mother would serve us children. The desert was usually sponge cake and custard and of course water to drink. There was a white linen tablecloth and linen napkins (we called them serviettes) and proper table manners, politeness and good manners were mandatory!

Boots also had a private lending Library and I think Mum paid a shilling a week for her membership. We always visited this Library after dinner to exchange Mum's book. When Dad went on his own to Shrewsbury he always changed Mum's book for her. He relied on the librarian to pick out a replacement for him as she seemed to know all her customers likes and dislikes very well. Mum was an avid reader and lost without her book!

After lunch, if the weather was fine and we were very lucky, we would visit the Quarry Gardens or wander along the riverside watching the rowers from Shrewsbury school. Unfortunately, all too often Mum wanted Dad's opinion on something she had seen in a store and we spent that precious hour trailing around the shops yet again before it was time to get home for milking!

When we reached Wenlock, the children were coming out of school and we would be told to crouch down and hide so that no teacher should see us skipping school! Since the teachers must have known we had not been in school I never quite understood the point of this exercise!

After we gave up the farm, any shopping expeditions were confined to Saturdays and generally we took the Midland Red bus which left Wenlock at 8am.

I remember one particular trip when virtually everyone on the bus ran to the shoe shop which I think was at the top of Mardol! We had heard that they had a shipment of 'Joyce' shoes which they would start to sell at 9am! 'Joyce' shoes were imported from the USA and their new flat wedge heeled shoes were all the rage – if you could get them! This may have been their first appearance in a Shrewsbury Store.

Of course, the line was already quite long when we arrived. Naturally, the townspeople had been there since dawn and several other country busses and trains arrived between 8am and 9am! Everyone was afraid that supplies would run out before we reached the front of the queue!

At 9am sharp the door opened, and four people were allowed inside. They all quickly came out again with a box of shoes which they proudly displayed to the hopeful multitude patiently waiting. Gradually, as more groups of four were allowed in we crept nearer and nearer the front of the line.

When our turn came at last, we realised why the turnover of customers had been so fast; the owner asked what size, produced two pairs of shoes which differed in pattern or colour, (they were all the new 'slip-on' flat wedge heel style), the customer chose which pair they wanted and paid in cash. I believe they were £5 which was a fortune in those days!

Only one pair was allowed per family and trying on was limited to a quick standing one legged slip on and off! Most people didn't even bother! Mum was delighted with her tan slip-on wedge although she only wore them for best because they were not a very comfortable fit! I believe my sister inherited them after a few outings and absolutely loved them.

Of course, Shrewsbury shops were our source for several special treats and making time to pick up our favourites was mandatory, no matter how important the main purpose of our visit to town!

Beddard's, the butcher near the bottom of Mardol, was famous for his 'Savoury', a kind of pate which was pressed into a large oblong pan and then turned out for slicing. We all loved it, for it provided a real change in our extremely limited menus. Mum would buy enough for a slice each for supper and, during school holidays, a pound of their famous home-made sausage for Monday dinner. During term time, we all had our main midday meal at school which meant our 'tea' was usually sandwiches and cake or something on toast or perhaps a salad. A favourite Sunday tea was salad which consisted of a box of mustard and cress, (occasionally we grew our own on blotting paper), shared between four bowls, topped with half a hardboiled egg and, of course, Heinz Salad Cream!

Morris, at the top of Pride Hill, were the only store that I remember making their own toffee after the war. There were two varieties, plain and molasses, and each piece was wrapped in a twist of wax paper with the store name printed on it. An early visit was essential as the toffees sold out very quickly! Toffees were favoured for their 'mouth-life' and those Morris's toffees stuck to your teeth like glue!

Morris's also produced meringues! Shaped like a flat desertspoon they came in white and pink and were very dry, sweet and crumbly. They were designed to be sandwiched together with a blob of cream, but we usually ate them plain! Because of their fragility, a bag of meringues could not be carried far. This meant delaying their purchase until just before we went home. All too often Morrisses were sold out by then! Even when we were lucky enough to buy a dozen, usually several had been reduced to crumbs by the time we reached home! But even those crumbs were incredibly good!

15. Wenlock, Our One-Stop Shopping Centre

Back then Wenlock boasted a retailer for our every need! Furthermore, they were prepared to cover every occasion when required. Thompson's still sold men's suits 'Made to measure'. Thompsons Ladies Wear carried a full range of clothing and immediately ordered in any requirements for special events.

My Mother often told us this story relating to my Grandmother's sudden death in 1933. At that time funerals were usually held within three or four days and full black mourning clothes were obligatory for all the family. Everyone else who attended the funeral wore at least a black armband if they did not possess full mourning clothes. The day after my Grandmother's death, Mum received a message that she was to be at Thompson's Ladies Wear by 4pm! She arrived to find her sister-in-law and future-sister-law already there.

With due ceremony, and after many condolences and the serving of tea, Mrs. Thompson brought out the three dresses she had ordered for them from Shrewsbury. As she already knew their size, each was specifically chosen. There were no alternatives! The

Seamstress marked up any alterations required and Mum was told her dress would be delivered the next morning! This was the first new dress Mum had had since her wedding three years before! Furthermore, its cost meant that it became her 'best' dress for the next several years! No wonder so many women wore black, it was all they had!

We had four bakeries, Harrison's/ Duckett's on the High Street, Gregory's on Wilmore Street, Duckett's on Sheinton St. and Massie's further up Sheinton St.

Each store had a speciality. Harrison's/Duckett's (I think Duckett was the baker and Miss Harrison ran the Grocers), sold teacakes on Saturdays. These were a big favourite with our family and Mum used to order them earlier in the week to make sure we would not miss out! About 4 inches diameter and thick enough to slice through the centre, we loved to toast them on our three-pronged extending toasting forks over the living room fire and spread with 'butter' for Saturday tea. (We always said butter but of course it was generally Stork Margarine).

The standing joke was estimating how far away Miss Harrison had stood to throw in the currants! Sometimes the verdict was 'Shrewsbury'! Essentially, dried fruit was virtually unobtainable except for about a pound (450 Grams), per ration book near Christmas. Poor Miss Harrison was lucky to have any to throw in from anywhere!

Massie's always opened on Good Friday morning to sell Hot Cross Buns fresh from the oven. Baked only on Good Friday morning, this was a once a year treat that tasted all the better for its freshness and rarity! Massie's had a small general store as well as the bakery.

Most folks at that time had very small ovens and cooking a large bird for Christmas was impossible. Fred Massie baked many

Christmas Dinners in his big bread ovens, and we would see and smell the results being carefully carried home just before 1pm!

Duckett's made cakes and yeast buns as well as bread. Their window would be full of trays of long finger like iced buns and various other cakes and pastries. Those iced buns were magnificent and the only ones I ever bought on those exceedingly rare occasions when I had both the permission and the cash to buy one!

Gregory's bread was low salt which produced a dedicated clientele!

The Breadman (who may have been Mr. Duckett from Duckett/Harrisons) regularly delivered fresh bread all around the town. We would arrive home from school to the smell of a fresh loaf of bread sitting on the kitchen table having been delivered during the day. In our teens, we loved to slice off two thick chunks and spread with Lyle's Golden Syrup before we tackled our chores!

We had two milkmen. Joe Lloyd delivered his milk by horse and cart. The milk was measured directly from the churn into the buyers' milk can. His cousin, Jack Lloyd had a bottling machine and used a mechanical milk cart. Jack's daughter, Beatrice made the deliveries all around the town. In the late 40's Derek Hill, (he had taken over the rental of the Brook House Farm from my Mother), also sold fresh milk (bring your own milk can) from his new milking parlour and dairy in the Stackyard on Sytche lane.

All our milk was unpasteurised and turned sour within a day or two, particularly in hot weather. No one I knew had a refrigerator and the common practice was to boil any unused milk in the evening to prevent its souring overnight. Should we forget, any sour milk would be set in the pantry on the marble slab (our cold spot) until it was solid. If this was poured into a cheesecloth and left to drip for a day or two it produced a ball of good cottage cheese!

Our Greengrocers were Perry's on the High Street and Higgs on Sheinton St. Their produce was limited to whatever was in season and Higgs generally purchased at the wholesale market in Bridgnorth or Wellington. When imported goods became available in the late 40's Wolverhampton market provided more choice. Our staple vegetables were potatoes, carrots, onions, beets, swedes, sprouts, cabbage and spring cabbage and purple sprouting in the Spring. Cucumbers were a treat and sold as halves! They were served in sandwiches after being sliced razor thin into vinegar! Tomatoes appeared for a short time in late summer. Mushrooms were wild and scarce, occasionally there would be lettuce but boxes of 'mustard and cress' or bunches of watercress were the standard salad greens.

Fruit was limited to whatever was in season. Apples, particularly Bramley cooking apples, seemed to hang about until the first of the rhubarb crop started to appear. With no temperature controlled cold stores, apples tended to become wrinkled and tough by Spring but were fine when they were peeled and cooked.

Some years Higgs would get a shipment of oranges in December. These were rationed to one orange per Ration Book and often turned up in the toe of our Christmas Stocking! After the war, more imported fruit began to appear, but it was very expensive and we had all gotten used to having our peaches canned! I remember seeing and eating my first banana and being totally unimpressed!

Flowers came from Cornwall, we saw small bunches of violets and daffodils, but most folk either grew their own or had little to spare for such luxuries! Growing daffodils on the cliff meadows in Cornwall was a large commercial enterprise until it was wiped out after the war by the cheaper imports from the Channel Islands and Europe.

Higgs store always reminded me of the descriptions I had read of Roman shops! It was basically a hole in the wall with the merchandise spreading out onto the pavement when extra space was needed. Any gamebirds or rabbits for sale were hung on hooks on the outside wall. It must have been very cold work for the assistants in the winter!

Perrys was run by two unmarried sisters who had inherited the business from their father. The called themselves 'Fruiterers' and seemed to have their supplies delivered. Their merchandise was primarily inside the shop with only a few items on display in boxes atop a wooden stand on the pavement. As a child, I was always fascinated with the fact that they sold lettuce and that the one sister's name was Lettice! The other sister's name was Aletha, also very uncommon!

Most people had at least a small garden and grew lots of their own vegetables and fruit. Gardens tend to produce too much or too little so bottling or salting away surplus was routine. There was always fear of botulism with bottling vegetables and the only vegetable I remember Mum bottling was tomatoes! However, we did salt down huge earthenware pots of kidney beans which were part of Sunday dinner right through to Spring!

Mr. Garbett on Sheinton Street, a bricklayer by trade, was an avid gardener and grew the most beautiful large Boston Lettuce which he sold for a shilling each.

Mr. Johnson, who looked after the town's water and sewage plants, provided our tomato plants each Spring from the myriad of self-seeded plants which flourished around the Sewage Plant at the end of the Bullring. Mr. Johnson had lost his toes in WW1 which meant that the points of his shoes turned up! He always got around by bicycle.

Two dear old ladies in Homer had a cow which they kept for their own milk and to feed a calf or two. When the cow first calved there was so much milk, they would make butter. This only happened about once a year, generally in the Summer. Terrified of breaking the law, they traded the butter surreptitiously at the back door! I remember walking down to buy some with Mum and how good it tasted!

One winter, (I think it was either 1942 or 1943) we had a huge snowstorm, and the CO-OP truck could not get to Wenlock to pickup our farm milk. We produced between eighty and a hundred gallons each day and most of that days' milk had to be fed to the calves or thrown away! Mum, whose mother had been a champion butter maker, dug out the old pans and big butter churn and made several pounds of fresh butter. Using the wooden paddles unearthed from our attic she created two small butter pats for my sister and I, each with a flower pattern pressed into the top. As it was against the law to make or sell butter, she gave most the butter away to friends around the town. Somehow the favour would be returned in kind for that was how most things worked in those days!

Even in the 1940's some Grocery stores were part of a chain! Mr. Martin managed Phillips in the High street and there was a CO-OP on Wilmore Street.

Lloyds, beside the Memorial Hall was owned by Thomas Cooke at the time of Queen Victoria Jubilee celebrations. Mr. Cooke was Mayor of Wenlock that year and he gave a large donation toward the cost of the clock tower in the Square as a commemoration of the Jubilee. The gossip around the town was that he had devised the gift as a means of preventing any buildings being constructed which would detract from his own location! This story still persisted fifty years later, I have often wondered whether there was any truth to the gossip or whether it was just another case of 'sour grapes'!

Lloyds, Evans on Barrow St. and Harrisons (of teacake fame) were all independent businesses. Several other shops sold some groceries although with the advent of rationing many found it difficult because, except for items purchased with 'points' and our sweet coupons we had to register ration books with one shop only. Points were used for things like canned goods and syrup. The number of points per item changed according to the national supply!

Upper High Street, Clayton and Graingers on left.

We had three butchers, Powell's, on the Upper High Street, Clayton and Grainger in Raynald's Mansions and George Langford on Sheinton St. all of whom butchered their own meat. Of course, from 1939 on, all meat was severely rationed by price. This meant you could have a larger piece of meat if you chose (or were offered) a cheaper cut! Offal and sausages were mostly not rationed but the butchers themselves tended to share out supplies among their customers.

Mrs. Connell on Wilmore Street sold some clothes and shoes, but mainly material, ribbons and lace by the yard, small rugs, and lino (linoleum)!

Pat Connell, her son used half the store for his electrician business. Their store sign read Chas. Edwards and I often wondered who he was! Many years later I learned that Charles Edwards was Mrs. Connell's father.

Tommy Thompson and his family had a Men's Drapers at 1 Barrow Street and his wife ran the Ladies Store opposite the George Inn. They had a newsagent / bookstore on Barrow Street too.

Confectionary and tobacconists' businesses were favourite small businesses, and we had several in Wenlock; Griffiths next to the George Inn, James opposite Barclay Bank, Dodd's by the Church and Garbett's with its quaint Bow Window, almost opposite the Gaskell Arms.

Noel Davies, our Saddler, won many awards at the west Midland Show and gave demonstrations there too. When I started high School, my new leather satchel was made to order by Mr. Davies. A few years later he made my first shoulder bag too. I spent some wonderful days watching and learning some of his techniques for my College Thesis on Shropshire Crafts. He was a true craftsman; watching him construct and stitch a horse saddle was an incredible privilege!

Mr. Woolley, opposite Barclays bank, was a carpenter and undertaker. His apprentice was Gerry Bowden. When my extremely tall Grandad Yates died, Mr. Wooley told the family he had some extra long oak boards put by just for the Gaffer! Living and dying was very much a village affair!

Mr. Woolley's wife was an extremely popular lady for she opened a Fish and Chip Shop in an old shed at the back of the carpentry business! It was the only one in town and she opened every Friday and Saturday evening. There was always a long queue! Scallops were extremely popular! They consisted of smallish potatoes fried in batter and were much cheaper than the battered cod. I think a bag of chips was 3d.

Mr. Austin ran a Barber's shop on Barrow Street complete with a Barber's red and white striped Pole. He regularly cut my hair into a short, bobbed style until I let it grow long enough to braid. He rented his upstairs room to a dentist who visited once a fortnight from Wellington. I only had the misfortune to use his services once – toothache might have been the less painful option!

There was a hairdresser on High Street I think, but most people used 'Back-Kitchen' salons for a cut and 'home-perm'!

Our chemist was part of Boots chain and was always well stocked. In the early 40's Dr. Bigley would mix many of his own medicines. Later on, as more products became available and new young doctors moved into town, a prescription filled by the Chemist became routine. My main memories of shopping at the Chemist was being sent to buy yet more indigestion pills for my father, who suffered greatly with 'indigestion'. Alas it turned out to be a grumbling appendix which finally burst with catastrophic results!

Burtons, on the High Street, was quite a large store selling everything from cigarettes, candy, newspapers, magazines and books, to knitting wool, embroidery silks, pens, pencils, bottles of ink and toys!

Some services which were routine back then have virtually disappeared! Some people did not wash their sheets, towels and tablecloths at home, they sent them to the laundry in Bridgnorth.

I believe Stentiford's on the High St. was the agent. They were also agents for one of the Dry Cleaners.

Tom Bache and his brother, distant cousins of my father, had a garage opposite the Gaskells Arms. As with all mechanics they were totally self taught which sometimes led to surprising results. After my father's death, my mother needed to brush up on her driving. Previously, like most farmers, my father had done all our vehicle maintenance. Uncle George offered to go out with Mum for some driving practice but suggested that Tom Bache give the car a good going over just to make sure there were no problems first!

The first lesson was to drive down the Bullring and turn by the old Quarry. Halfway back they suddenly shot into in the ditch! After the cursing (George) and the tears (Mum) were over, they discovered that the 'Big End' had dropped out whatever that was! George and Tom thought it was a great laugh, but I don't think Mum ever truly trusted a car again! To be fair to Tom, such things must have seemed trivial to a man who had been in the Flying Core in WW1 regularly flying over enemy lines!

Mr. South ran a Garage between Ashfield Hall and the Back Lane. His wife, a tall slim lady was quite a character, a very independent thinker in a town where the worst threat of all was "What will people say!"

One day Mrs. South explained to my mother her strategy for survival whilst running a household which included her husband and three young boys, who were all generally covered in oil! She had invented her system when her maid had disappeared into the much better paying munitions factories at the start of the war.

It was quite simple! She set out three large tables in their main room. All the clean dishes and cutlery were piled on one table. They ate at the second table. The third table held all the dirty dishes! When the first table was empty and the third table was full, the whole family was corralled into washing up and reloading the first table. This had to be completed before the next meal would be served!

"I feel that managing the rations, cooking good food and making sure they have clean clothes come Sunday is more than enough for one woman and I am not prepared to become a slave to any man!" declared Mrs. South to any who dared question her solution!

Although many shoe repairs were completed at home, our village cobbler was an essential part of the community. Mr. and Mrs. Jones' little shop opposite Ashfield hall was always buried in shoes and boots awaiting repairs. Leather soles did not last long, and all new shoes (except ladies' dress shoes) came to Mr. Jones for a line of metal cleats or hobnails around the sole and heel. When the cleats wore thin the shoes came back for replacements!

They were Agents for Clark's shoes, but any supplies which did arrive were gone almost immediately. Shoes were made to last as long as possible and handed down through the family. As the smallest in our family, when my sandals became too tight, mum just took a razor and removed the leather from above the toes. Yes, my feet got wet when it rained but at least my toes didn't pinch!

We had two ironmongers, Forby's on the High St., and Smith's on Barrow St. At some point in the late 40's Mrs. Bessie Smith opened another general ironmonger store opposite the Church. She was quite a character, a chain smoker, ex teacher and mother to four children. Always with a smile on her face, generally some salacious gossip, and a ready supply of 'fags and matches tucked up under the leg of her knicker elastic, she brightened many a dull day. In contrast, her husband was a quiet introspective man who rarely had much to say!

For many farm repairs, our most important resource was one of our Blacksmiths, either Evans on Victoria Road or Choppy Hanson on St. Mary's Lane behind the George.

Although new furniture was virtually unobtainable during the war and used or 'Utility Furniture' was our only option, Phillips Furniture Store on Smithfield continued to operate although much of his stock was second hand. When Nellie Smith opened a China Shop on Barrow St., we really became a full-service community!

16. The Great Glovemaking Enterprise

In 1944 or 1945 some of the WI ladies were determined to make themselves some warm fur backed gloves. Since each glove would require one rabbit skin, it was decided to start the project when there would be plenty of skins available at the same time. By some miracle, they had managed to obtain some soft pigskin which could be used for the palms, the fur backs they would process themselves.

In those days wheat grew quite tall and was cut with a binder which deposited a long line of sheaves to be picked up and 'stooked' to finish drying out. The rabbits had been enjoying a summer of copious food supplies and shelter among the golden wheat stalks. Rabbit snares placed around the edges of the fields had provided many folks with rabbit stews, but rabbits are prolific breeders and by harvest time farmers were intent on reducing their population before the winter. Some fresh meat to supplement our meagre rations would also be welcome.

Each field was cut in a circular pattern towards the centre and of course the rabbits among the stalks had no escape except to travel further into the wheat! When only a few more circles remained, every good marksman would stand around the edge of the field and wait for the moment of mass rabbit breakout.

Safely corralled beside the gate I covered my ears as the hail of gunfire burst forth. Soon it was all over, and the happy hunters headed home with several brace hanging by their legs from each gun barrel. Those they could not use themselves went to the local butchers and provided funds to pay for the cartridges and maybe a pint or two at the pub that night.

Rabbit provided a good meal for a family. Despite the need to carefully remove the occasional buckshot as one ate, it was a luxury in a world where our meat ration at one point was so small it was photographed beside a matchbox!

Soon the ladies had all the skins they needed. Mrs. Head tanned several skins, including two for my mother. It was a very smelly process and she worked in their garage (it stood at the end of their garden) in hopes the wind would disperse the stench ASAP! I was glad it was not happening in our backyard!

My first close up look at the process came when the skins were already stretched and nailed to plywood sheets which were propped around her garden in every available sunny patch. We were recruited to help 'scrape' and soften the pelts. I did not enjoy the job!

The ladies met at the Stork meeting room to cut the leather and stockinette lining. This was an arduous process since it required the utmost skill to make the leather provide enough glove palms. Even so some seams appeared in unusual places! I think the lining was recycled from old worn-out coats.

Sewing required a good thimble and a sharp needle and many a lady bore the marks of her nightly struggles! My mother resorted to an awl to hammer tiny holes in the leather and rabbit skin as one of us stretched the material over a block of wood!

Their reward came on Christmas Day when every lady proudly wore her new leather gloves to Church. Several folks asked the group if they would make them a pair; they would be happy to pay! Alas, not a single glovemaker was prepared to tackle another glove ever again.

17.Our Quarry Playgrounds

Linden Walk which FW Yates helped plant in the 1870's, leading to the Windmill and its quarries. Great for scooters and bicycles! Alas they were officially forbidden!

During the late 30's and for most of the 40's, the myriad of old quarries around Wenlock were virtually derelict. Even when operations resumed, they tended to be relatively small scale in the immediate Wenlock area and had little impact on our freedom to wander the old workings.

During quarry closures nature busily worked its magic over all except the most recent excavations and so we inherited a playground of humps and bumps of arid land partially covered with wiry grass clumps, tiny wildflowers and large scrabbly bushes of rosehips and blackberries.

The older defunct quarries were covered with bushes and larger trees which clung to the ancient manmade hollows. The resulting mulch had softened the landscape and provided homes for greater plant growth to such an extent that it was only in later years that I realised that some of the 'woods' or 'coppice' where we played were actually old quarry workings!

The 'woods' beyond the games ground on the flank of Windmill Hill and Shadwell Quarry itself, were favourite areas for playing Cowboys and Indians, Hide and Seek and other group games. Feeling very courageous, we occasionally explored the old kilns at Shadwell and threw stones in the deep Quarry Pool. The wilderness of land that stretched from Shadwell kilns to the Farley road was riddled with sheep paths which wound among the random hummocks and hollows.

In the deepest valley, immediately behind the Windmill itself, was quite a large group of large pine trees. This was a favourite place for gathering large pinecones to fill an empty summer fireplace or as kindling for future fires. A large cone always hung outside our back door as a weather predictor! Cones opened wide in dry warm weather and closed tightly on damp drizzly days.

Many of us were avid fossil collectors! The old quarry workings behind the Windmill were a treasure trove of large and small fossils which had already been broken free of the ancient rock. I had an enormous collection of fossils, carefully arranged in old biscuit tins on layers of cotton wool. Every fossil was unique; shells were the easiest to find, those of plants or leaves the rarest and consequently, the most prized. My friend, whose father worked in the coal mines near Dawley, had a huge coal fossil leaf!

Today, all that area and several additional fields have been quarried far into the ground and the whole area has become a vast blue lagoon with only the town face of our Windmill Hill and the ruins of the Windmill itself left for future generations to enjoy!

Today, we would have been able to learn so much more about our finds on the Internet. I envy my granddaughter's knowledge of the universe and astronomy. At twelve years of age, she is accessing research information which would have taken us many hours of study even if we had had access to a university library!

During the war, rosehips were collected and processed into rosehip syrup. The old quarries and many of our hedgerows abounded with white dog roses in the summer months and they were easily found, although the vines were long and often intertwined with nearby vegetation. Their thorns made picking a prickly process. Taller people with longer arms had a definite advantage!

Oranges were virtually unobtainable throughout the war – we were allowed one per ration book just before Christmas. Concentrated orange juice was provided for young children via the family clinics. However, Rosehip Syrup, an excellent source of Vitamin C and a home-grown product, was used to supplement our diet. I don't remember tasting it myself, expect we got our vitamin C from the potatoes which formed a large part of our dinner every day!

I remember picking rosehips as a family. We all picked into the one basket and I believe we were paid 2d or 3d a lb. It was very much a war effort and a matter of pride to help with the WI total. My contributions were minimal – I was simply too small to reach 99% of the hips!

Blackberry picking during our High School years was a vastly different matter. High Schools had two weeks more summer holiday than Primary schools. We used those weeks to earn as much as possible picking blackberries! Mum, an Infants' School teacher, had already returned to work and we were free to spend our days out picking with friends. Our favourite spot was the old Shadwell Quarry. Here it was possible to fill a basket during the morning and return to fill a second basket after lunch.

At 6pm each evening we carried our precious cargo up the Shrewsbury Road to Percy Chamberlin, a Small Holder whose farm buildings stretched along the left-hand side of the road just past the turn to Church Stretton. Percy had a large set of scales where he weighed our baskets with the berries inside and wrote down the weight. Most evenings several women and older children were already in line.

Percy seemed to have a sixth sense, (possibly it was a weight versus volume estimate), for any recalcitrant picker who had added a few pebbles! Such suspect baskets were shaken and inspected thoroughly! First offences were a warning, a second offence meant the culprit's produce would no longer be purchased! With virtually no other means of making some extra pocket money this was indeed a catastrophe! No one tried it a second time!

Our basket was emptied into one of several tall narrow topped wooden barrels which were lined up against the wall. Each barrel would be half filled with berries before being covered with its wooden lid. After weighing the empty basket and subtracting its weight, we would be paid 3d or 4d a lb for our berries.

Each night all the barrels would be given a good shake down and filled even further. This went on for several days until, even after the most vigorous shaking the barrels were filled to the brim with blackberries! Only then was the lid nailed on ready for shipping.

About once a week Percy pulled his trailer, loaded with barrels, to the station and put them in the Goods Van for delivery to Roberston's factory in Birmingham where our berries would be turned into Roberston's Bramble Jelly. A new supply of barrels would be waiting for him on the platform.

Robertson's Bramble Jelly was extremely popular! Hearing the discussions about the discovery of Penicillin from a mouldy petri dish, I often wondered if the jelly contained an antibiotic effect! Surely the berries at the bottom of the barrel must have been mouldy, possibly even fermenting towards wine! Mum assured me it would have been sterilised thoroughly during processing and in fact, fermentation had long been used as a food storage methodology and was quite safe!

With a plentiful supply of Mum's homemade jam including bramble jelly, we never actually bought any jam and very little marmalade. Unfortunately, this meant that we took ages to collect enough paper golliwogs to send away for even one golly pin! In fact, I do not remember ever reaching the required 50 stickers!

Blackberry picking was a major supplement to our meagre allowance and as such was always saved for a special purchase. One year I earned enough to purchase a length of blue crepe and dress pattern with which I made my first teenage party dress!

Mr. Martin, Phillips Grocer's Manager, used to tell the story of a young employee boasting that she had a new 'creep' dress. His reply? "Have you got 'sood' shoes to go with it?"

Making fun of such a mispronunciation was common and we all suffered such 'jokes' on occasion! In fact, Crepe had only just become fashionable again, and I expect she had learned the name from a Woman's magazine. The latter provided our main source of knowledge about the latest ladies' fashions in those days.

Just beyond the Windmill Hill on the Farley road, the Buildwas and Sheinton roads form a fork with the left-hand road heading slightly uphill through the old quarry workings to Sheinton and the Buildwas road heading downhill and marking the separation between the old quarry and farmland. A narrow shortcut beyond the old Quarries completed the triangle!

In my childhood, the initial 'Y' fork was marked with a sturdy barrier about twenty-five feet in length which consisted of a shiny metal cylindrical bar about two inches diameter threaded at six-foot intervals, though four or five concrete posts.

The furthest bar from the fork had the highest ground clearance. It was a perfect location for somersaults! Consequently, not only was the bar extremely concave but the ground beneath had been worn into a deep gully!

It was mandatory to stop and perform, or attempt to perform, several somersaults whenever we passed!

Being undersized and unathletic, I frequently returned home with my navy-blue knickers well coated with green grass streaks and a layer of earth, proving once again that I could not complete a somersault around that bar no matter how hard I tried!

The old quarry waste land which lay across the top of the Sheinton road had been unused for so many years that it was covered with small trees which included many hazelnut bushes. I think we called it Norry's quarries.

I was fascinated to read in Glyn Williams' Book 'Much Wenlock Limestone Quarries' that before that land ever became a quarry it may have originally been known as Nutgrove Hill. Obviously, the hazelnut trees survived the quarry operations sufficiently well to be able to reclaim the area when the quarries left!

The lower hanging clusters were picked and eaten long before the outer shell hardened. Family Sunday afternoon trips were required to collect at least a few mature hazelnuts from the higher branches to save for the Christmas season.

When we lived a few miles from Wenlock, at Arlescott, there was a huge beech tree at the end of our lane and, in the autumn, the ground beneath was covered with beechnut husks. Unfortunately, many were quickly flattened by passing traffic or covered with mud or dust! Consequently, on weekends, we often walked across the fields to Barrow and on into Willey Park where we could find sweet chestnuts and beechnuts in the green parkland. I never remember taking any home! They were too good eaten fresh sitting beneath the trees whilst fresh nuts continuously rained down around us, and the squirrels busily garnered their winter stores!

In later years when we had moved back into Wenlock, we would sometimes cycle to Willey Park. Windy days produced the best supply of freshly fallen nuts, but alas windy days and cycling don't mix! This meant that all too often the potential harvest was not thought to be worth the ride and some other activity would be deemed more fun.

Conkers were prized possessions in the Autumn term. The best Horse Chestnut trees in Wenlock were at the top of the Cutlers yard near the train line. When I was very young Grandad Yates told me that the field was named 'Cutlers Yard' because a long time ago that field was the site of the cutlery factory!

In Spring one of these trees had pink blossoms which were exceptionally beautiful but only produced small weak conkers. The conkers from the white blossomed trees were much larger and harder.

Playground Conker battles reached epic proportions! Each prized conker was threaded through with a length of string long enough to wind around your hand and leave about a foot of free string. The aim was to hit your opponent's conker in such a way that their conker split but your conker stayed whole. The longer a conker lasted the greater the prestige of the owner!

The name of the conker changed with each victory and the proud owner of a 'Niner' or Tenner' was a giant amongst us, until some little kid with a small hard conker shattered that glorious possession to smithereens!

We used conkers to make doll's house furniture as well. Using pins to frame legs and chairbacks, we wove brightly colored wools tightly through the pin frame to create solid sturdy and very pretty chairbacks and legs. Dolls to fit such tiny chairs were made of wool shanks, tied to resemble the human form and finished with a paper circle face.

Although we had few commercial toys or games we were never bored. Someone was always seemed to have a new suggestion- 'Why don't we....?'.

And our next great adventure would begin

18. The Old Beam

This blackened beam above the cavernous fireplace in my grandfather's home was instrumental in attracting me to letters and words from an incredibly early age. As Grandad and Uncle George helped me decipher the names and dates, I learned so much of our family's 'recent' history. Grandad was born in 1861 and had known every person named except his Grandfather, the first George and his Grandmother Mary. This is not surprising considering that his grandfather had been born in 1765 and Grandmother in 1773!

The Yates family had lived in the area for centuries and everybody in our town seemed to be a 'cousin' or distant relation'! In those days when ordinary folk stayed close to home and even a distance of 10 miles was viewed as 'away' most people married within the village or nearby hamlets

Today it is fascinating to look back through our family tree and discover that, although the average age of death in Britain was around 40-50 over the period 1700 to 1900 the fact is that those who did survive lived well into their 80's and 90's. There is a tablet in Shifnal Church commemorating a Mary Yates who died at the ripe old age of 129 having remained active until the last five years of her life!

Looking back over my paternal grandparents to 4 generations the average age of death is 87 for the men, rather less for the married women. Surprisingly, unmarried daughters frequently lived into their late 80's and continued to live in the family home and work alongside their younger relations.

'Retirement' was virtually unknown among country people! Farmers and tradesman alike continued to work with the help of those children still at home until the end.

In 1834 when George Yates was 69 years of age, his wife Mary was only in her mid fifties and they had four young children still living at home. Some years before they had opened The Horseshoe Inn on Sheinton Street (probably in the front portion of their home) as a supplemental income and insurance during the recession after the end of the Napoleonic Wars in 1815.

When the tenancy of the George and Dragon Inn in the centre of town and close to the Market Hall became available George jumped at the chance of the larger business. It could be easily managed by his wife and daughters and provide them with a secure future! It would also keep his daughters, Ann and Alice, at home to look after their parents as they aged! George himself continued to run his Blacksmithing business on Wilmore Street with his son William and sundry apprentices.

George had been apprentice, journeyman and then Master-Blacksmith since the tender age of twelve. Blacksmiths were key members of society at that time. All nails and chains were handmade, all carriage and cartwheels were fitted with iron tyres and the vast numbers of horses providing the primary source of power for agriculture, for transport and for pleasure needed to be shod frequently.

But the job required great physical strength and long hours. The George Inn would provide him with supplemental income as he passed more and more of the heaviest work over to his apprentices.

Proudly he burned his name on that fireplace beam for all to see and admire - G. Yates 1834! The larger premises enabled him to expand his home- brewing and cider-making which became an established tradition until the final Yates gave up the licence in 1957.

George died in March 1847 just before his 82nd birthday but his wife Mary continued to run the business with her daughters Ann and Alice until in 1850 when Ann/ Alice was granted the licence. A.Y.is burned in the top left-hand corner of the beam!

Now in 1850 Ann was 32 years old and stepping out with Henry Hopton. Alice was 30 and stepping out with Thomas Ainsworth of the Brook House Farm. But there was no question of either marriage whilst the girls were required to look after their mother and brothers and run the Inn. In Victorian times it was expected that a daughter's first duty was to care for her parents and unmarried brothers!

Although their mother died in August 1851, the girls hung in there for nearly three years! Thomas had married in 1847, he and his wife Mary established a hairdressing business further up the High Street and operated it until the end of the century. Only George was left at home!

It seems that having a wife was essential to running an Inn! George's trade was 'Painter and Glazier' and he seems to have been in no hurry to marry and take over the Inn!

In 1854, first Ann and then Alice married their sweethearts. However, Alice continued to run the Inn! The married woman laws at that time demanded that the licence be assumed by her husband, Thomas Ainsworth, but the family carried on as usual and no new name appeared on the beam.

At last, in March 1857 George married Jane Norris of Cardington and immediately carved G.Y. 1857! I often wonder if there was family pressure to get a move on as Alice was pregnant and finding it more and more difficult to run 2 homes!

George seems to have had lots of interests. He was leader of the Wenlock Brass Band, a member of the Ancient Order of Foresters who had their headquarters at the George Inn, was active in everything going on around the village including the Annual Olympic games, and kept up with his trades of Painter and Decorator and Glazier!

Upon his death in 1892 his wife Jane took over the licence and burned her name under Alice.

Family stories imply that Jane was not the friendliest of Mother-in-laws, despite her son Fred (FW)and his wife Kate having five children before her death in 1900! However, the lure of the old George Inn worked its magic once again as FW Yates took over the licence and added his name below his father. He was to become the longest licensee, 1900-1944.

By this time George and his wife Gene had virtually been running the business for 10 years. It seems changing the licence was not high on anyone's priority list! Finally, George was able to carve his name, the third George Yates at the George Inn. Alas George suffered a stroke in 1945 and, although he recovered enough to walk a little with crutches, he remained an invalid until his death in 1948. His wife, Imogene Atkinson (Gene) Yates who had been a teacher in Wenlock for many years before marriage, virtually took over the business in 1945 but the licence did not change until George's death in 1948. 'I.A.Yates 1948' is carved below her husband.

For the next 9 years Gene ran a very successful business with the help of Charlie Jones and her father James Cartner and FW Yates. She finally retired at the Michaelmas Quarter in 1957. FW Yates was 96 and had lived at the George for all but 10 years of long eventful life! But I will tell you his story another time!

The George Inn with 1 Barrow Street in distance. From 1866 to 1903 this was James Bodenham, Tailors. They were my Great grandparents. James was Mayor of Wenlock in the late 1890's

WENLOCK INN TO LOSE FAMILY NAME

—AFTER FOUR GENERATIONS OF LICENCE HOLDERS

THE name of "Yates" has been associated for so long with the George and Dragon, Much Wenlock that it will seem strange when another one appears over the High Street entrance to the inn after Sept. 24. For on that day Mrs. I. A. Yates, the present holder of the licence, retires and ends a family connection with the house that has continued without a break for 123 years. It was in 1834 that the George and Dragon—one of three free houses in the town belonging to the Wenlock Abbey estates—was occupied by Mr. George Yates as the first member of the family to hold the license. He was followed in 1850 by Miss Alice Yates and seven years later his son, Mr. George Yates, took over. He held the licence until 1892 when he was succeeded by his wife, Mrs. Jane Yates. On her death in 1900 her son, Mr. Fredrick William Yates, grandson of the first Mr. George Yates, took over the inn and held the licence for the longest period of all—until 1944. He then handed over to his son, George, who died in 1948. Since then the latter's wife, Mrs. I. A. Yates, has been the licensee.

MRS. I. A. YATES

Although he relinquished the licence in favour of his son, Mr. F. W. Yates still lives at the George and Dragon and at the age of 96 is the town's oldest inhabitant. He has led a very active life and has taken a keen interest in public affairs. For nearly 10 years from 1937 until 1946, he was a member of the Wenlock Borough Council, and for the same period was chairman of the War Memorial Board. He also served on the old Wenlock Board of Guardians and on the Gaskell Recreation Ground management committee. Up till five years ago he was trustee of the Court Albert Edward of the Ancient Order of Foresters, a position he had held for 40 years. Joining the junior branch at the age of 16 he is the oldest member of the Court. The George and Dragon is the headquarters of the Order.

MR. F. W. YATES

As a church bellringer for 70 years, Mr. Yates was one of those who rang the curfew till that ancient custom ceased in Much Wenlock about 1910.

In his younger days he played cricket, football and tennis, and was an ardent supporter of the Wenlock Olympic games founded by the late Dr. W. P. Brookes. For a number of years he was a member of the drum and fife band which Dr. Brookes started.

Mr. Yates and his wife, who died in 1933, had a family of four sons and two daughters, of whom one daughter survives and now lives at Cheltenham.

On her retirement Mrs. Yates, with Mr. Yates, will live at 5, The Crescent, Farley Road, Much Wenlock.

Stained Glass door panel created and etched by FW Yates.

19. Our Annual Fair

At some point, during those long days of double summertime, our Annual Fair snuck into town almost unnoticed. The travelling country fairs liked to pack up after closing on Saturday night and move to the next village over the weekend. There they would park their waggons and settle in for a few days rest and repair before setting up the rides and booths.

Like the circus, the Fair used the field opposite the Gasworks. This meant that our first knowledge of its arrival often came on Monday morning when the Mathews children arrived at school. Mr. Matthews was the Manager of the Gasworks and the family lived in the house beside the large round gas storage tower. They had enjoyed an exciting weekend checking out precisely which rides might be included this year and were the 'go to' source for information that first morning!

Our Fair was always open Thursday and Friday evenings and Saturday from about Noon. We could talk of nothing else in the playground and dreams of hoped for future exploits filled our thoughts.

For such an important occasion, we were allowed to raid our Piggy Banks and of course we would have our pocket money on Saturdays too. Compared to the Fair, our weekly visit to Dodd's sweet shop held little appeal! Come Saturday afternoon it was simply a race to the Fair!

As we scattered among the attractions, we were busy checking out every single Ride and Booth and, of the greatest importance, how much they cost! Only then were we ready to decide where to spend our precious limited funds.

The Dodgem Cars were always the star of the show and a magnet for all the adults and any children who could reach the pedals. Unfortunately, they also cost a whole shilling, way out of most kids' price range! Those lucky enough to have an older sibling or parent aficionado were often able to hitch a ride as passenger. Everyone wanted to drive their own car, but the passenger could be any size!

I was never a Dodgems fan, far too bumpy, but in terms of entertainment they provided the best show in town. Folks rammed each other with enthusiasm, crazy driving was the rule rather than the exception. For many folks, this was their only driving experience! Naturally, my big brother and his friends loved it and paired up for ride after ride until they ran out of money!

My favourite game was Roll-a-Penny! An octagonal meshed booth was surrounded with eight narrow funnels, just large enough to take an old British penny, which sloped downwards onto a flat blackline chequered board where each square was slightly larger than a flat penny.

Most of the squares carried an amount ranging from 1 penny upwards. Some squares were blank! The most desired squares which paid 1 shilling, a florin (2 Shillings) and half a crown (2 shillings and sixpence) were in strategically impossible corners!

The easier more central squares were either blank or paid 1d, 2d, or 3d! A very, very few paid sixpences! In order to win, my penny had to land completely inside a square without touching any of the black lines!

The first big decision was which slot to use! Some slots were deemed to be luckier than others! Although it was fairly easy to win your penny back or perhaps land on the 2d. or 3d. in all the years I played 'Roll-a-Penny' I never saw anyone win more than sixpence! Winnings were always short lived since they only represented 'free' extra rolls and almost everyone seemed to stay until all the money they had left was spent!

'Hook a Fish' was another favourite. A large blue lined trough of water surrounded the operator. This was stocked with flat gaily painted fish each with a ring in its nose. Armed with our purchased fishing line we attempted to hook as many fish as possible. Some of the fish carried a marker indicating we had won a goldfish!

Those beautiful goldfish were proudly carried home in the old jam jar provided. We did have a goldfish bowl at home, but those fish never seemed to live for more than a few days. When plastic bags came along the jam jars were replaced with plastic bags which were much more vulnerable to breakage! All too often that prized goldfish gasped out its last breath on a dusty pavement where it provided a tasty meal for any passing cat!

The gloriously decorated 'Merry-Go-Round' was the centre piece of the fair. Keeping time with the lilting music, the magnificent steeds gracefully rode forever up and down and round and round! Each horse carried its own unique decorations and seemed to portray such individual characters that it required considerable thought before deciding on our chosen ride. They were much more my speed than the Bumper Cars!

One year a new attraction was called the Jelly Wobble! This comprised a walk, or rather a wobble along a narrow track which snaked back and forth around a trailer bed. This pathway shuddered and jerked continuously and holding on to both sides was essential! I found it hilarious watching those who had paid for the privilege of being virtually shaken to death, but my first ride was also my last! As they say, 'It just wasn't my cup of tea!'

I loved the swing-boats and would stay on them until either I ran out of funds or, more often, willing partners! The operators liked their boats to be moving to catch more trade. Should no new customers be waiting, they would frequently allow us to swing until other customers showed up or, more rarely, until we were too tired to pull the rope any longer!

During the war years coconuts had disappeared from the British market and so the Coconut Shy had morphed into throwing rings over bottles or whatever other substitutes could be found to emulate the coconut!

The first time I ever remember seeing a real coconut was at Wenlock Fair soon after the war. My brother managed to win one and, carrying his precious coconut, he returned home triumphantly!

The next morning, we all assembled in the backyard to for the 'Opening Ceremony'! First, Bryan drilled two holes and drained the 'milk' into a cup. It resembled slightly dirty milky water! Nevertheless, the cup was passed around with due ceremony and most of us took a sip!

Bryan used a sledgehammer to shatter the coconut itself. It bounced around quite a lot before it finally shattered! Chunks of the shell with the white flesh still attached were shared amongst us and we used our ever-present pocketknives to cut out chunks of the white flesh.

Alas, after all the effort and huge anticipation, both the flavour and the texture were very disappointing and most of us happily passed our chunks on after just one bite!

In many ways, the real excitement of the Fair lay in the sheer reality of wandering about the booths and rides, almost drowning in the cacophony of shrieks and yells which punctuated that raucous background music, and just looking at everything!

Alas, all too soon, it was time to go home for supper and our fair was over for another year! By Sunday evening our village had settled back into its usual peaceful calm and only brown foot-trodden pathways around yellowed squares proved the reality of our Saturday memories! Those memories enhanced by our vivid imaginations filled every thought as we relived 'The Fair" and all agreed that we could not wait till next year!

But don't forget! We must all make sure to save a heap more money!!!!

20. Our Long Walk Home

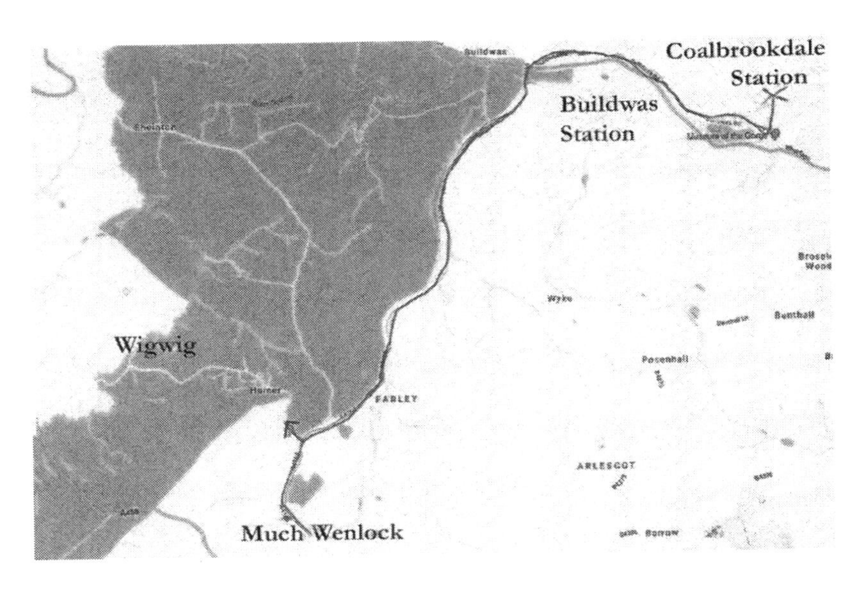

Distance from Coalbrookdale Station to Wenlock Church is 5½ miles and over 300ft climb.

The Winter of 1947 remains epic among British winters! An Internet search will provide many photographs and detailed accounts. My sister and I had started Coalbrookdale Grammar

School in September 1946. Sue would be 12 years old that November and I had had my tenth birthday in June and was small for my age. Such were the vagaries of the entrance examination rules which allowed every child two attempts to pass to Grammar School.

We were the first cohort of the new system. Prior to 1946, there were scholarships available, but it was also possible to pay for a Grammar School education regardless of academic ability. The sudden closure of this option created enormous stress for children of families who had traditionally paid to send their children to Grammar School even if they did not obtain a scholarship.

We joined the new entry level classes of 1A and 1B. There were thirty-one students in each class, the largest one-year intake in the school's history. My brother was already in the 5th form which meant that for one year we were all in the same school. Little did we realise how important that fact would prove for our survival that winter!

January 1947 was very cold with many frosty days and nights, but no one was prepared for the snowstorm of January 22/23. We had caught the train as usual that morning with light snow falling. By lunchtime there was already a significant accumulation and the snow and wind was increasing.

The older boys went to see the headmaster to ask if we could be sent home early on the 1 pm train as they feared the line would soon be blocked with snowdrifts. Mr. Herring hooted with laughter at the very thought that tough 'country' kids were trying to get out of school early for 'a bit of snow'.

The snow continued to fall heavily all afternoon. At 3.15pm when school finished, we all ploughed our way up to the station which was about a half mile from the school. The station master greeted us with the news that the 3.30pm train had not yet left Wellington and we were in for a long wait!

This news was followed about 15 minutes later with the announcement that all trains were cancelled until further notice as drifts covered portions of the track! Men were being sent with shovels to clear the track and, since it was still snowing hard, it was going to be a long job. In fact, it was likely there would be no more trains that day!

Thirty plus children crammed into the small waiting room as we waited for the oldest boys to map out a plan. Obviously, we would have to walk the 5 ½ miles (9 ½ K) home to Wenlock. Those who lived further on up the line could stay with friends in Wenlock overnight.

Fortunately, most of us had been sent to school in wellington boots with our mandatory leather lace-up Clark's shoes in our heavy leather satchels. Our school uniform dictated that all the girls wore navy gymslips and knickers, white blouses, and navy wool sweaters. The boys wore school blazers over their sweaters with short grey pants until Senior school when long grey flannel trousers were allowed. We all had knitted woollen knee-high socks held up with elastic bands and a navy gabardine mackintosh and school hat – caps for the boys and berets for the girls. School blazers and long navy school scarves complete with tassels and bands of green and white, completed our uniform. In those days, bare knees were a way of life for all of us!

At this point it is worth remembering that we had grown up in a world where houses were heated only by coal fires and, since the coal ration was only a hundredweight (112 lbs or about 50 Kilograms) per week, these fires were generally only lit in the evening. Regulations ruled that school heating could only be turned on from November to March. However bad the weather at

least one window was always open in our classroom and even our homes. Everyone wore a wool vest and all the girls and even some women wore a 'liberty bodice'. This was a bulky padded garment which provided a great deal of warmth. The optimum temperature for schools was I believe 61F/16C but with constantly opening doors, draughts etc. the only really warm place in school was right beside one of the radiators.
The snow continued to fall heavily as we formed a long crocodile behind the largest boys and started our long trek home. Although we would be following the main road there was no expectation that we would meet any traffic! Certainly, there was no road clearance of any kind and I do not remember meeting a single vehicle!

Since my sister and I were the smallest we were at the very back of the line and walked a well stamped out path through the deep snow which was already severely drifted between the steep hedgerows. Our big brother had taken our heavy satchels and he walked the whole distance with three satchels slung across his back. The other older boys followed suit divesting the smallest children of their load.

We left the station about 4pm, first walking down past the school, (now firmly shut for the night) then on to join the Buildwas road. The first mile or so follows the river and is fairly level. But once we turned left across the river bridge, we faced an uphill climb of about 440ft /133m over a 4 mile stretch as the road climbs up Farley Dingle.

Just past the bridge is the lane to Buildwas station. Here we stopped to wait the outcome of an argument for heading to the station, about half a mile walk, or continuing towards Wenlock. In the end, only two girls decided they would go to the station. I did not envy them! No big boys would break track for them and perhaps they would be stuck there all night! The rest of us were going home, however long that took!

And so we plodded on once more! My world was reduced to my sister in front of me and the snowy walls on either side. Steadily we trudged onwards and upwards through Farley Dingle. Farley Train Halt was deserted. No railway lines were visible through their thick snowy layer.

Eventually we reached the turn to Homer and Wigwig. It would be all downhill from here. Waving goodbye to the kids who faced another two-mile downhill walk to Wigwig, we started down into Wenlock. We created quite a sensation when we reached the first houses at the Crescent and children started dropping out of line as they were welcomed home and hurried into the warmth. Poor Mrs. Corbett was horrified to hear that José and her friend had turned toward Buildwas station!

At last, it was our turn! We still lived at 1 Sheinton St. (the Brook House Farm) and arrived home to a cold and empty house. Our mother was stuck somewhere unable to get home from her teaching job in Broseley as all the buses were cancelled. But we had made it! We were home!

Bryan set a match to the living room fire and then lit the paraffin space heater at the back of the room. Fortunately, we had a gas stove for cooking and were soon wrapped in blankets around our small fire, nursing steaming bowls of bread and milk.

The snow continued to fall steadily, and I think it must have been about 7.30pm when an icy blast from the front door heralded Mum's arrival! She already knew something of our adventures as José and her friend had eventually made it to Buildwas station. Our Mother was among the crowd of commuters from the Severn Valley line who packed the small Waiting Room hoping that a train to Wenlock would eventually get through!

Mum had experienced her own adventures. She had walked from Broseley down to Ironbridge station (via Broseley Wood and the Iron Bridge) and caught a train to Buildwas where she had been stuck until at last one train made it as far as Wenlock!

The next day was Friday and we all had a day off school. Most of the outlying villages around Wenlock were cut off and the news bore the grim stories of a country brought to a standstill by the continuing heavy snowfalls. We missed a lot of school that winter due to either the weather or 'the flu'.

Most days our mid-morning bottle of milk (free to all school children) arrived at our desk with the foil cap perched on top of a column of frozen cream. We had two choices – use the foil cap as a spoon to scoop off the 'ice cream' or wait until it softened sufficiently to push a straw into the bottle itself and drink the milk below. Eventually the cream would soften and sink and could be stirred into the remaining milk thus creating a kind of sludge which could be drunk from the bottle.

Men dug a tunnel through the lane to Callaughton, a small village two or three miles outside Wenlock. Callaughton was only reached via ancient sunken lanes which had quickly filled with drifts. Between over six-foot-high walls of snow the tunnel was just wide enough for two people to pass. I remember one brilliantly sunny, bitingly cold Sunday afternoon when we walked almost all the way to Callaughton and back just to experience such a unique phenomenon!

Sledges were dragged from barn lofts and saw sterling service on the Walton Hills. Uncle George had two sleds, The Flying Scotsman carried four passengers and we kids put it to good use! The other sled was reserved for adults. It was wide enough for two to sit abreast and carried six. Amazingly it also had a brake!

By March we were all used to the continuous snowstorms and it seemed almost a surprise when warmer air suddenly arrived, and all those mountains of snow began to shrink. Travelling home from school that day all the talk was of the likelihood of getting in one more weekend of sledding.

Imagine a chattering group of children coming down Station Drive to Sheinton street only to find that street had become a torrent of water hissing and bubbling its way down into town. Even the pavement (sidewalk) was flooded and only the uneven state of the road allowed us to wade along the edges!

We knew only too well what we would find at the Brook House! The floor of our house was about 6 inches lower than the pavement and, when street flooding occurred, water poured into our house. Such flooding had happened so often that flanges either side of the front door frame had been constructed to hold a barrier board to try to reduce the water flowing in under our front door.

When we arrived home the water already several inches deep in our hall and dining-room. Our oval drop leaf dining-table was fully extended, and the two armchairs and the carpet were piled on top! The back-kitchen floor drains were securely blocked with bricks holding down thick pads of old towels. These were necessary since our old house was built almost over the brook and when the latter was in flood such drains could quickly transform into bubbling smelly water fountains. Grandad Yates had anticipated the flood and sent men down to take the usual precautions!

We too knew the drill! When we arrived home the water had receded sufficiently to stop pouring in from the street. But the water in the hall was level with the top of the step. Wading through the mess we parked our coats and satchels on the staircase and gathered the galvanised hand-basins from the back

kitchen.
With three kids taking turns bail out mucky flood water over the barrier board we managed to get the level down to the 'mopping stage' by the time Mum arrived home an hour and a half later!

But I still remember the steamy stench that seemed to permeate the whole house for several days. We left the Brook House at the end of March that year. The old house certainly gave us a memorable and rather smelly send-off!

21. The Thrill of Icecream!

It is strange how memories are built of small and infrequent events long after day to day happenings have faded into oblivion. Perhaps our memory sees no need to store the mundane daily routine, but special events are red letter days which must be remembered in all their glorious detail. The return of Lyons Ice Cream to Gregory's store in 1946 was just such an event!

The big red freezer chest with 'Lyons' emblazoned across the front, together with a sign declaring that Gregory's store was the official supplier of Lyons Ice Cream, had remained in place beyond the wicket gate throughout the war. This rickety old gate stretched between the ends of the long counters lining both sides of the store. Always kept firmly closed and bolted, that gate provided the only means to move behind the counters or access the living accommodation beyond. How I longed for just a peek inside that dusty red freezer!

Even though I had no memory of the taste of ice-cream, that big red chest freezer fascinated me. I believe it may have been the only freezer in the town. I have no memory of ever seeing another.

The making of ice-cream had been banned during the war years and even when production began again there were strict regulations regarding the ingredients. Cream was not available until the end of rationing. Since our milk was untreated, the cream rose to the top and my mother would skim this off into a small jug to be served over bottled fruit for desert. The remaining milk must have been equivalent to our current 1% or perhaps even 'Skim Milk'.

Until the demise of our local passenger service in the 1960's we Wenlock kids travelled by train to and from Coalbrookdale Grammar School. The line from Wellington continued beyond Wenlock through Longville all the way to just outside Craven Arms and children from as far away as Cardington travelled by train to Grammar School in Coalbrookdale.

There must have been about thirty children from Wenlock who caught the 8.30am train and returned at 4pm. From 1946 or 7, every two or three weeks, a frozen food container full of Lyons Ice-cream was shipped to Wenlock in the Guard's van. Imagine our excitement when the guard hopped off the train at Coalbrookdale station and someone spied the distinctive red container in the Guard's van!

Gregorys' Lyons Ice-cream is on board!" was the cry! Glum faces identified those unlucky children who travelled further than Wenlock. The unluckiest kids were those who still had a long cycle ride or walk from Wenlock station. My friend Maureen (who was to achieve fame later in life for completing the Thousand Mile Land's End to John O Groats walk) still had a three-mile cycle ride to Shirlett. Running home to beg for ice-cream money was impossible for them as it would be sold out before 6pm closing time!

We Wenlock kids tumbled from the train at Wenlock station, waving our passes enthusiastically towards the ticket collector as we raced for home! Our mission was to conjure a threepenny bit out of our parents or be permitted to raid our own piggybank. Our excitement alerted the whole town and very soon a large cohort of children were running towards the station to meet the porter with the important red container loaded on his handcart.

Like the Pied Piper he led a steadily increasing crowd of children down the Station road, under the railway bridge and along Sheinton Street.

The faithful and growing escort chanted quietly but with great enthusiasm.

" I scream, you scream, we all scream for ice cream! "

Gregory's store lay opposite the Church and next door to The Stork Hotel. The narrow double front doors flanked by two large bay windows sat above 4 wide stone steps. As far back as I can remember those enormous windows were virtually empty. Occasionally a few loaves of bread would appear for an hour or two, but for the most part it seemed that what little Gregory's had for sale was sold long before there was time to put it in the window.

Always known as Gregory's, I never remember seeing Mr. Gregory. He was the baker and seemed to prefer remaining behind the scenes. His wife was assisted by Gertie Dawes. When I was small, I always thought they were sisters! Both were elderly and seemed to have trouble walking. Wearing voluminous garments and matching grey fuzzy hair they generally shuffled about in carpet slippers. I have no memory of ever seeing either Mr. or Mrs. Gregory or Gertie about the town or at any social event.

To us kids Gertie was the Boss and the one who kept us all in line. Mrs. Gregory was smaller and gentler. Gertie yelled at us and we listened! Her gentler companion would beg us to 'Shush Please!'.

Gregory's main business seemed to be the Bakery. Their bread was special in that they used very little salt. Every loaf was usually spoken for before it came out of the oven. I imagine the store had been a larger portion of the business before the days of rationing.

In my memory, the counters and shelves were always almost bare. A desultory selection of half full sweet jars and the odd loaf of bread were scattered, seemingly at random, along the shelves. A fat red sausage about four inches in diameter and up to a foot long generally sat on the bacon slicer, occasionally there was a pan of faggots in gravy on the counter. Sometimes I would be sent with a cooking bowl to buy four faggots and gravy for our supper. Faggots are a mix of pork liver, heart and caul mixed with breadcrumbs and herbs and cooked in a rich brown gravy. Gregory's' faggot balls were about two inches in diameter. They were extremely tasty when reheated with lots of gravy and served with toast.

The double front door had large, frosted panes and both doors were ceremoniously opened so that the porter could carry the ice-cream container beyond the wicket gate and set it on the large red freezer. Immediately he left, Gertie locked the doors!

Now began the seemingly endless wait for the ladies to check their delivery and move everything into the big red freezer. We were some of the lucky children who lived close by, and, as the crowd grew, we jealously guarded our place on the steps! Soon half the kids in town were scrabbling around on the stone steps and the pavement beyond.

Eventually, Gertie unlocked just one side of the door and announced she was ready, and we better behave ourselves if we wanted serving! The half door provided only a narrow entry and even we children had to enter single file. Once inside we formed an orderly line against the rarely used right counter.

As we dutifully waited, clutching our treasured octagonal golden threepenny bits, we inched forward until at last we could hand our money to Mrs. Gregory and receive our prize from Gertie! Our treasured reward would likely be rejected, perhaps even ridiculed by children today!

Each ice-cream came individually wrapped. It consisted of a circle of ice-cream about 4 cm in diameter and three cm deep. A band of waxy thick paper which surrounded the sides was removed by Gertie and dropped in the waste bin as she balanced our prized purchase in a specially designed cone. The ice-cream sat firmly inside the cone and was held in place by intruding cone flanges. The cone itself was much larger than that little circle of ice-cream and was designed so that the ice-cream was almost impossible to dislodge. It was quite a thick wafer crust and tasted almost better and lasted longer than the ice-cream itself, a fact which did not escape our notice!

The ice-cream taste resembled rather poor-quality stale frozen custard; the texture had more similarity with sweetened cardboard than any ice-cream available today.

Such details were of little interest to us at the time. With either very distant or possibly no previous memories for comparison, actually having an ice-cream in our fists was pure delight! Such an epoch-making event was certainly not to be diminished by any comment or criticism of either taste, size or quality. The joy of possession reigned supreme.

The cones were quickly sold, and the chest shut until 5.30pm. when wafers went on sale to adults only. For this purpose, anyone who was working full-time was deemed to be an adult. Since School leaving age at that time was fourteen many teenagers could buy wafers too. Wafers cost sixpence!

I think that these wafers must also have been delivered unwrapped and separated by the waxy thick paper. In my memory, Gertie always handed them over already placed between two wafers. They were quite small, about 8 ½ cm by 4 ½ cm and perhaps a centimetre thick and definitely far inferior to our wonderful cones!

I was quite sure that, for once in our life, we kids had certainly had the better deal!

22. A Film Crew Comes to Town

Rumours that a film crew might be coming to town thrilled young and old alike! Wenlock in 1949 remained an old fashioned sleepy little town where life had always followed a predictable path!

Surprises were few and far between and this one seemed to be incredible! Folks oscillated between disbelief and anticipation as we all waited for this unbelievable event to be confirmed or denied!

Happily, the rumour was confirmed in our weekly paper! The film would be made by Michael Powell and Emeric Pressburger, names we all knew and admired for the wonderful movie 'The Red Shoes' which had been released the previous year. 'Our film' would be 'Gone to Earth' who's author, Mary Webb, who had spent her youth in Wenlock and described it as "A little Rip Van Winkle of a town which fell asleep in the Middle Ages…."

My grandfather remembered Mary Meredith (her maiden name) very well and had read all her books! The Meredith family sat in the pew in front of the Yates family in Church. Although Grandad would have been in his twenties and Mary just a small girl it seemed they both had a sense of fun which resulted in a surreptitious game played during long boring sermons. Mary had long braids which temptingly fell over the back of the pew and onto Granddad's small bookrack. When the sermon was particularly boring, he gave those braids a slight tweak! Mary's resulting quick smile and flick of her braids improved the sermon immensely!

For us children the possibility of a job as an extra during the Summer Holidays was all we could think about. Children would earn £1 and Adults 30 shillings for each day they were used. This was a veritable fortune!

Notices went up announcing auditions in the Library Room at the Corn Exchange the following Thursday. The children could audition at 5pm and Adult auditions would follow at 7pm.

School dragged interminably that day until the final bell released us to sprint up to the station. There was an audible sigh of relief when our train arrived on time. It seemed that the old engine had never struggled harder or crawled more slowly as it puffed up to Wenlock!

At long last we creaked into Wenlock Station. Barely waiting for the train to stop, all the doors burst open as we catapulted onto the platform. Whizzing past the ticket collector, we raced home to drop our satchels, grab a slice of bread and syrup and a glass of water, (my favourite after school snack) and run down to the Corn Exchange! Everyone wanted to be at the front of the queue! Who knew how many would be hired!

There are several steps at the back of the open ground floor of the Corn Exchange which led to the Lending Library and the stairs to the offices above. The whole area quickly filled with chattering, giggling children. We were experts at queuing, and each knew their exact location in line! No queue jumping allowed!

At last, the one half of the narrow double doors opened, and we were allowed to squeeze inside one by one! Our audition involved no more than a quick inspection and taking our names and addresses. All our fears of missing out were groundless! Everybody was added to the list! Whether we would actually be called to work was still a question.

Gene (an Innkeeper) and FW Yates in costume

From the conversation around town, it seemed that all the adults who auditioned later were hired as well. The Wheatland Hunt members were recruited, especially the ladies who could ride side-saddle, and farmers with older carts or buggies were in great demand.

Each days' shooting requirements were posted the day before and my Grandfather and Aunt Gene from the George Inn worked the days that the Wenlock Market Day scenes were being shot.

Today the George Inn Market Room Door is again the main Inn entrance from the High Street. But in 1949, the Inn entrances were along the George Shut and the Market Room served both as the family dining room and a banquet and meeting room. So the first time in my life that I saw the Market Room street door and the iron gates under the Guildhall wide open with folks going in and out was for the filming of 'Gone To Earth'.

Many adults and children were called to work the Wenlock Market Day scenes. I think those of us not working had the most fun as we were able to scoot quickly around the town generally getting underfoot but satisfied that we had not missed a single thing!

My most enduring remembrance is of watching Jennifer Jones as 'Hazel' buy herself a 'new' dress at Raynalds Mansions. The latter had been transformed into a Used Clothing Store. The 'new' dress was formfitting and a lovely shade of green which perfectly enhanced her wonderful almost luminous eyes and elfin expression as she danced her way out among the traffic!

Gene Yates with friends enjoying the action!

At last, the Wenlock scenes were finished and my mother, sister and myself were on the list for the following day. We had to be at the Corn Exchange for costumes and makeup at 6.30am! I wore a deep blue dress which reached below the knee, with white stockings and a voluminous apron, a poke bonnet and my own long braids trailing down my back. Most of the girls wore similar outfits. Funnily enough I have no memory of makeup!

We all travelled by bus to Hughley, where the 'Travelling to Market' scenes were to be shot. One of the carts was a group of children on a Sunday School outing and this was where I had expected to spend my day.

Emeric Pressburger, a rather gruff figure with a foreign accent, of whom we were all in awe, strolled across to our group of children, and asked everyone to line up against the Church wall. He wandered up and down the line, staring at each of us for a few minutes, then beckoned myself and another boy to come forward. We had been chosen to be the children of a farmer and his wife and ride in the back of their buggy. Our seats faced backwards, and Mr. Pressburger wanted each of us to kneel up and peak around our parents' shoulders as the cart travelled along the road. We practised and reshot the scene for hours! A spotted black and white dog was supposed to run along under the cart. Alas he would not behave well enough to suit their requirements and eventually the Director gave up on the dog!

Over a year later we all went to the Granada in Shrewsbury to see the finished film. Imagine how thrilled I was to see a closeup of my face! Admittedly the cut was so short that merely a blink would cause the audience to miss my big moment, but I knew it was there and that was all that counted!

From mid-morning onwards, the dinner wagon emitted wonderful smells and was obviously ready to serve us all around the noon hour. Alas the film crew were totally engrossed in their work and it seemed that not one member of the cast had the nerve to mention lunch!

We worked on, shooting and reshooting with the scents of a wonderful dinner wafting around us. At last, just after 2.30pm, Pressburger himself headed toward the lunch wagon, calling a break as he walked. Naturally, he was first in line, followed by the main cast with all the extras and general workers waiting behind!

All too soon, filming began again and continued till nearly 6pm. They were long days! Providentially, the weather stayed partially sunny for the entire two or three days we worked in Hughley! When we finished and collected our pay, I did not expect to be called again as the crew was moving on to the Stiperstones area.

Luckily, the entire film crew were staying in the Wenlock area for the August Bank Holiday weekend to attend the Carnival Parade and Olympic games. Our Maypole Dancing was a real hit and the Director decided he must include it as part of a background shot somewhere!

This desire led to all the Maypole Dancers being bussed to Lord's Hill above Snailbeach for several days in succession. Once there, we plaited and unplaited our maypole numerous times! Alas, only the plaited pole lying on its side made the final cut! Such are the fleeting flashes of potential fame in the film industry!

The friendly little Baptist Chapel at Lord's Hill became our home base where we endeavoured to entertain ourselves during long hours of doing nothing! The Hymn Books and the Bible were the only reading material available, but we all loved to sing! Hymn singing was an important part of school life which we all enjoyed. Soon, an impromptu concert materialised as we sang our way through those old, tattered Hymn Books!

Whenever the call for 'Quiet Please' was heard, an adult would erupt in our midst signalling us to stop! Silent as the ghosts of people past who seemed hauntingly close upon the Stiperstones, we waited for the 'All Clear' before continuing on exactly where we had left off!

Several of the girls could harmonise and, as the days wore on, I suppose we sounded better and better with quite unexpected results!

It transpired that the quality of the singing recorded by those riding the Sunday School Picnic waggon at Hughley was not very loud. After listening hour after hour to our 'concert' it was decided that we should record some hymns for later dubbing into the Hughley tape.

A large sound baffle was set up outside and we were marshalled into tight formation in front. Now there is vast deal of difference between belting out hymns just for the fun of it in an enclosed room and singing to order before a large audience! Outside we sounded much quieter and I think we were all somewhat shell shocked at our sudden fame! We had a large audience too, for the whole crew gathered around to enjoy our impromptu concert! They recorded several hymns, I often wondered whether they ever used them. In the final movie, the few seconds of singing did not sound that good, was it us or was it the original Hughley recording? I suppose we will never know!

Dame Sybil Thorndyke, who played the minister's mother, had been unwell and did not come to Shropshire at all. Since her character was swathed from head to foot in black, a double was used for all the distance shots. I believe Mrs. Bradford was her double at first but she was not available for the Lord's Hill shoot and my mother took her place. Mum's main claim to fame was that they used her voice calling 'Supper' from the Minister's house beside the Chapel. Seemingly she had the correct 'Shropshire Dialect' emphasis!

All too soon, our thrilling summer was over. We collected our last pay packet and life returned to normal in our ancient sleepy town. The film crew were history! They moved on to other venues and I suppose recruited other extras.

They had boosted the revenue of many local businesses and given many unemployed adults and children an encounter with transient wealth beyond their dreams.

For myself, an avid reader, I found my mother's copy of Gone to Earth and fell in love, not so much with the story, but with Mary Webb's incredible ability to paint with words!

Familiar scenes that had always given me pleasure became even more seductive! Over the next few months, I managed to borrow and read all her books as I realised that Mary Webb had captured the soul of my home county in a manner that spoke of knowledge, empathy and understanding. Her perception and understanding of people and the natural world about them must have evolved in her childhood around Wenlock as she roamed my very own countryside. It was an intoxicating thought and gave me a desire to enlarge my horizons that has enriched my whole life.

Footnote: The Full Cast of 'Gone to Earth' is available on the Internet. Typing in the name of any one of the extras, none of whom (to the best of my knowledge) ever played a part in another film, brings up the legend: -"...... is a Film star known for 'Gone to Earth'!!! "

Surely such a legend is proof of the often wide discrepancy between an Internet 'Truth' and 'Reality!'.

23. A Remarkable Woman

Gene Yates lived in Wenlock from 1912 until her death in 1980. Imogene Atkinson Cartner became a Yates by marriage and I knew and loved her as Aunty Gene. She was an impressive role model to follow, a truly remarkable woman!

Born in Portinscale, Cumberland in 1893 and moving to the Peak District of Derbyshire in her High School years, she retained an intense love of those mountainous districts her entire life. But Wenlock was home!

Gene obtained her first teaching post at Buxton High School where she was Gym Mistress at the tender age of 16. In 1912 she obtained a teaching post at Much Wenlock School and remained a teacher there until her marriage to George Yates in 1933. A tall slim active woman she was very fond of sports, a team member of her High School Netball Team and founder and coach of Wenlock School Netball Team. Her future husband, George Yates, was also an avid sportsman, goalie for the local football team and they were both enthusiastic tennis players.

George and Gene had a long courtship, as was quite common in those days. Their marriage was precipitated by the death of George's mother in 1933 as this removed the need to establish their own home. Gene retired from teaching, (mandatory on marriage in those days), and moved into the George Inn where she undertook the role of Innkeeper's wife and care for her father-in-law, FW Yates, who continued to be the nominal licensee until 1944.

Adept at all facets of the business, she had scant patience with any potentially obstreperous customers! Gene knew all the customers! She had either taught them or their children and was known for being a strict disciplinarian. Under her rule potential troublemakers were swiftly evicted and patrons were informed in no uncertain terms when they had reached their limit!

The 1940's brought large crowds of American Servicemen who were based in the area into town. The George was renowned for its home brewed beer and homemade rough cider and perry (which is made from pears). Frequently the old Inn was so crowded it was standing room only in the bar!

As had his father and grandfather and great grandfather before him George brewed beer every Monday, mild one week and bitter the next. The wonderful smell of hops permeated the whole town on those Mondays. Cider was pressed every September; the cider apples were brought in from Herefordshire. My first taste of fresh apple juice was from a glass held alongside the crusher in the George backyard! I remember 8 or 10 huge barrels of fresh cider lined up to cure along St Mary's Lane opposite the Cider Press Yard each September. Following the cider-making pears were pressed to produce a smaller batch of Perry.

George had served throughout WWI, spending most of the war in Salonica and then in Egypt and Palestine with the Motorboat Section. During WW2, he was a Captain in the local civil defence unit and Gene trained with the Auxiliary Nurses.

In 1945, George suffered a severe stroke which left him unable to speak and partially paralyzed. It seems strange to think of this today with our modern hospital system, but Gene nursed George at home with the help of the district nurse! George was a big man and customers often helped when lifting was required. The little private sitting room facing the street beside the George Shut was converted into his bedroom and Gene took over all the management of the business and gradually nursed George back to health. He regained the ability to talk, although his speech was slow and slurred, and eventually could walk a few steps, and be comfortable in a wheelchair.

The indomitable Gene decided a holiday would do him good and, with the help and accompaniment of the district nurse, took him to Llandudno for a week by the sea in 1947 and again in 1948. By this time, Charlie Jones was an indispensable member of the team together with Gene's father who had retired to Wenlock in 1940.

Alas in late 1948 George suffered another stroke, this time it was fatal. After George's death Gene continued to run the Inn and look after both her own parents (at that time they had a cottage on Barrow Street) and her father-in-law. She became even more active in the British Legion and worked extremely hard to achieve the building of the Legion Hall on Smithfield Road. George and Gene had been founder members of the Wenlock branch of the Legion in 1935.

My sister and I stayed at the George for a couple of weeks in 1949. My mother had had a very severe bout of flu and Dr. Holden said she had to go away for a complete break before he could allow her to return to work. Susan and I continued to live in our own home, but we went down to the George to sleep. Gene always had our supper waiting – a thick bread and jam sandwich and half a pint of cider! Rough cider packs a punch and we both slept like logs every night! It was the first time we had either of us tasted alcohol!

Gene created a wonderful teenage experience for all of Wenlock youth when she became a square-dancing enthusiast and organised and called for Square Dances every Thursday evening from 6.30pm to 8.30pm at the new Legion Hall. Circular skirts and flouncy underskirts became all the rage and I still retain fond memories of how much FUN those evenings were.

Once Gene's mind was made up, she persevered! After George's death Gene decided that she would learn to drive! All her friends drove and had done for years but she herself had never held a driving licence. First George and then her father had always driven their big old car. By this time new drivers had to pass a Driving Test before they could drive without an experienced driver beside them. Previously, one had simply purchased a Drivers Licence. Anyone who started to drive in the 20's and 30s had simply learned the basics from the salesman on a quick trip around the showroom area and were free to drive home!

First Gene had her father teach her. She failed the first and second test! She enrolled at a Driving School and failed the 3rd, 4th, and 5th tests. By now she was getting somewhat annoyed and declared she would keep trying until she did pass! I believe it was on her 12th or 13th try that she finally succeeded and continued to drive for the rest of her life!

Giving up the licence of the George Inn which the Yates family had held since 1830, in September 1957, Gene retired to the Crescent where she continued to make a home for both her father and father-in-law. Her father-in-law died January 1958 and her father in 1962.

Despite the ten-year difference in their ages, (Annie had been a student at Wenlock School when Gene joined the teaching staff), Annie Reynolds and Gene had been close friends for many years. They had long planned to live together when they were both free.

Annie's father and mother had already passed on and Annie was living at Ashfield Hall by herself.

With the development of the St Owen's road estate Gene and Annie built their retirement bungalow together at 1 St.Owen's Drive and lived there for the rest of their lives. Together, they visited the Oberammergau Passion Plays, (which occur every ten years) three consecutive times and travelled extensively.

At home, they remained actively involved in all Wenlock events. Gene's main interest continued to be the British Legion. Starting as inaugural secretary in 1935, she served in various positions throughout her life and ran the Poppy Campaign for over thirty years. Gene died in 1980. A truly remarkable woman, she had lived her entire life with zest and enthusiasm, no matter how great the obstacles she faced.

24. Our Treasured Cinema

The old Market Hall in the centre of Wenlock town has seen many changes over the centuries. In 1919 the addition of a large front entrance closed off the hall from the elements and turned the old building into Wenlock Memorial Hall.

Since then, the Hall has provided Wenlock with a town facility for various functions. At some point in the 1930's it became our cinema every Friday and Saturday evening with a matinee every Saturday afternoon. In those days, we did not go to the movies, we went to the pictures and this makeshift temporary conversion supplied the only regular entertainment in town.

The high timbered ceiling provided plenty of room for a large screen against the Wilmore Street wall and the 'stage' at the opposite end was converted to a 'balcony'. It held four or five rows of padded theatre type seating with steps up from the side of the stage and a centre aisle. Some Balcony seats could be reserved and were expensive. I believe in the late forties/ early fifties they were half a crown! Since the balcony was a flat stage, only the front row really had an unobstructed view of the screen. However, patrons were nearer eye level which, with a padded seat and backrest, formed a comfortable viewing area. The back row of the Balcony was particularly popular with courting couples!

Immediately in front and below the screen were three or four rows of backless wooden benches set out with a centre aisle. These were always crammed with shuffling chattering children who had each paid sixpence for the privilege of craning their necks back at an impossible angle to follow the on-screen action.

The main hall was filled with stacking chairs set out in orderly rows either side of a centre aisle. I remember these seats as being one shilling. They were popular with the teenagers and younger adults.

Those who considered themselves employers, skilled tradesmen, civil servants, teachers etc. or could afford the extra cash, generally paid for a softer balcony seat.

In my memories, which are primarily of the 1940- 1955 period the show routine never varied. Sargeant Dodd, our village policeman, was in charge. An usher was superfluous, since all the seats, except for the first balcony row which could be reserved, were on a first come first served basis.

The ticket booth opened about fifteen minutes before each show and in those pre-television days it was usually a full house. The front of the queue consisted entirely of kids clutching their sixpence determined to get the best seat on the bench! But for some 'special' films, even the adults' line could be quite long.

Sargeant Dodd's commanding presence alone was sufficient to keep the wriggling front benches in order until a raucous blast of loud music heralded the start of the first picture! There were no commercials! The program consisted of a 'B' movie, generally about an hour long. This was followed by the Pathe Newsreel and finally by the main picture.

Westerns, Comedy Films, and Sitcom Style Romances were extremely popular 'B' movies. The front benches comprised an active participatory audience. Bad guys were booed, heroes and heroines cheered, and every chaste screen kiss greeted with a chorus of raspberries or loud popping sounds produced when a finger was sucked and then popped from the lips with great enthusiasm!

The newsreels provided us with action shots of notable events like Royal Weddings and State Events and current hostilities like WW2, the horrors found in the German camps and all the other smaller wars of the period – Kenya, Malaya, Korea, Suez. Nowadays we take such footage for granted as visuals of the latest atrocity or war fill our TV screens almost hourly. Back then, it was thrilling, astounding, scary and frequently almost beyond belief.

The feature film came last, after a short interval.

Between each segment, Sergeant Dodd strode up and down the aisles enthusiastically pumping his sprayer which was full of DDT. There were no pre-filled sprayers at that time. The one commonly used resembled a-Heinz Beans can, with a cylindrical handle holding the pump attached to the side.

This routine spraying during the show was still happening in the late 50's! DDT use was not banned in Britain until the 80's. Since we did not have mosquitos, I assume the enemies were fleas, general infections like colds and flu and probably Body Odour! Prior to the 1950's many homes relied on tin baths in the kitchen and Saturday night bath night and clothes change was still the norm.

Mrs. Bessie Smith, the Ironmonger on Wilmore Street had been a teacher in the Liverpool Dock area during the 1930's. She often told me this story of her experiences. Apparently, in the late Autumn, many of the slum children would be stitched into a body warmer made of cotton batting. This remained in place until the return of warmer weather in the Spring. As you can imagine the aroma reached a significant level!

One little eight-year-old named Billy was particularly aromatic having suffered from several bouts of diarrhea. At the end of January Bessie sent home a note with Billy asking very politely if it would be possible to replace his batting as it was really very unpleasant in the classroom. The reply was prompt and pithy!

"My Billy ain't no rose. You larn im not smell im!"

Our Wenlock Cinema was frequently the only social event of the week for Wenlock children. We had a Guide and a Scout Troupe and a large Boys' Church Choir. But most of us made our own fun playing around the Games Ground and the Windmill. Instant fame surrounded those kids fortunate enough to have 'been to the pictures' as they regaled their friends with an account of the weekend's Western or comedy. Romantic stories received short shrift with the younger crowd for the most part as they were deemed to be very boring!

For newly released films or a special treat we would sometimes go to the Granada in Shrewsbury or the Majestic in Bridgnorth. These positively opulent establishments actually had a real sloping Balcony, sumptuous plush red fold up seats and a lady who came around during the interval with a tray of snacks!

Unfortunately for us, my mother thought that most films were a waste of time and our visits to the cinema anywhere were rare. Exceptions were made for all the Shakespearian classics and Michael Wilding films. The magic of 'Spring in Park Lane and Maytime in Mayfair stayed with me for many years!

I vividly remember the first film I ever saw! It was 'Beyond the Blue Horizon' and was in technicolour. The story escapes me, but I cried buckets when an elephant fell over a cliff and was too upset to watch any more! I think I was 6 or 7 years old.

After that we did not go again for a very long time!

The first Television program I ever saw was the crowning of Queen Elizabeth in June 1953. Our Math teacher, Mr. Thompson, had just bought a Television which may well have been one of the first in Wenlock! A school holiday was declared for this momentous day and Mr. Thompson invited all his Wenlock students to come to his house and watch the live broadcast of the Coronation.

We crowded around the huge wooden 'cabinet', which boasted a tiny screen about eight inches by six inches, watching the fuzzy, faded, flickering Black and White images. With intermittent technical breakdowns, the whole event was broadcast and lasted several hours! Although I would not have missed it for the world, it was definitely an extremely sorry affair compared to the gorgeous technicolour Newsreel shown in Wenlock Cinema the following weekend!

25. Our Christmas Party

For Christmas 1944 Mum decided we would have a big children's party for all our friends. This would be a reciprocal invitation for all the birthday parties we had attended and much more practical than individual Birthday parties!

We were thrilled to be having our own party at last and planning the great event consumed most of our thoughts for weeks before! The biggest priority for us was the need for a huge Christmas Tree! We had not had a tree the previous two Christmases and our small pre-war trees had been planted and were growing nicely in the garden. We all agreed that reusing one of these was out of the question! They were far too small!

Our big brother, Bryan, decided he knew exactly where we could get a tree and to that end, we all set out one Saturday morning just a week or so before the planned party. He led the way as we toiled up over the Windmill and down into the big stand of pine trees which filled a deep ravine right below the Windmill itself.

Those tall dark pines towered far above my head! The lower branches were pretty ragged, but Bryan explained we only needed the top six or eight feet of a tree. Reassured, we climbed a neighbouring hillock and solemnly inspected each tree searching for that one special tree with the perfect top!

At last, we were all agreed, one tree would be absolutely perfect! Bryan hoisted the saw on his back and started to climb. Our dining room ceiling height would only allow for about a six-foot tree, so Bryan had a long climb! Eventually he reached a point where the tree started to sway with his weight, and he had to hurriedly descend to a more stable perch. We heard the rip of the hand saw as he began to saw with one hand even as his other arm was wrapped about the trunk beneath his cut!

With my sister and I watching anxiously, it seemed to take for ever, before at long last our future Christmas tree hurtled downwards! Bryan let out a yell as his perch swung wildly for a few seconds and he enjoyed a wild ride before things settled down sufficiently for his descent!

Closer inspection of our prize indicated that it was still far taller than our ceiling! However, we lugged the whole thing home and presented our prize to Mum! She was thunderstruck and terribly upset at the risks Bryan had taken. When the dust settled, Marion, our landgirl, helped Bryan cut it down to fit the dining room and trim the branches back to a more acceptable width. The whole thing was wedged with stones and soil into a large, galvanised bucket and set up in triumph before our Sheinton street window. We had our tree!

A trip to the attic produced a box of decorations saved from pre-war years. Before too long streamers were strung across the room and concertina like silver paper balls and coloured fans danced above our heads. The tree ornaments were pretty sparse, but we did have lots of half burned candles in the tiny clip on candle holders, a beautiful silver chain and delicate coloured glass balls. The magnificent star was hoisted to sit just below the ceiling, and we thought the whole effect was splendid! Our own handmade paper chains filled any gaps. Above all it was ours!

The following day, we persuaded Mum to take our Sunday afternoon walk to the only holly tree with berries that grew on our farm. It was not a large tree and sat in the hedge overlooking the Homer road. But, every single year that small tree was loaded with berries and 1944 was no exception. Our haul was sufficient to decorate each picture frame and make a trail across the mantel. In addition, every size of brass candlestick, (and we had lots), received their own individual sprig and even the copper kettles spouted holly sprigs! The delicate white Goss China bust of Queen Victoria wore a necklace of holly as she gazed out upon our Drawing Room through her thin glass dome.

At last, the great day dawned! Susan and I spent the morning wrapping a gift for the 'Pass the Parcel' game and helping to open out and lay our big oval dining-room table.

All such parties in those days followed a similar genteel pattern!

Generally, as soon as all the guests had arrived, a couple of very sedate games, perhaps Blind Man's Bluff or Find the Ring, would be played before we all sat down to tea.

Several ladies, roped in as helpers, kept order and we were all on our best behaviour and very much aware of the need to keep our party attire as pristine as possible! The wonderful tree was duly admired, and a promise given to maybe light the candles later!

The table was covered with two white handmade lace tablecloths and place settings for ten children. The centre piece was a white rabbit blancmange sitting in a sea of red and yellow jelly. Most parties had a chocolate blancmange shape, but we did not like chocolate blancmange! There were fish-paste sandwiches, jam tarts, slices of ginger cake, buttered 'Harvo' slices and little currant buns. 'Harvo' was a chewy malt bread speckled with a few currants that we all loved. The Christmas cake was a sponge cake with a smear of icing and the treasured Christmas Cake ornaments arranged on the icing. As usual, we all drank weak tea!

The ladies prescribed a game of 'Pass the Parcel' while the table was cleared. Duly instructed we sat in a circle on the hearthrug. The game involves passing a parcel around the circle until the music stops. Whoever holds the parcel at that moment can take off just one layer of paper! Since we had no music, one of the adults facing the window and with their back to the ring, called 'stop' every few seconds. It was very boring, even though we ourselves had wrapped the parcel enthusiastically only hours before! Inevitably, with such painful slowness, that pathetic package shrank smaller and smaller. The winner would be the person who revealed the prize, but I have no recollection of even finishing the game!

Our 'caller' suddenly announced "Oh dear, here comes trouble! Now we are in for it! Its your father-in-law!"

Jettisoning the ragged little parcel, we all rushed to the window to see my beloved Grandad heading down the street towards our house with a large sack on his back! Decorum and keeping clean was forgotten as we ran to open the front door and escort him into the Living Room.

The supervising ladies simply threw their hands in the air and retreated to the kitchen! 'Old Gaffer' Yates' reputation for stirring up mayhem was renowned!

Gathered around our own pied piper we waited with bated breath as he rested his sack on the table and started digging around as though he had no idea what on earth might be in that big old sack. At last, he seemed satisfied, and lifted his head to survey the sea of expectant faces surrounding him.

"Ok! Line up shortest to tallest and we'll see what we have here!"

Each reach into the sack produced a small papier-mâché trumpet. As the children grew bigger so did the trumpets and my brother, the last in line, received the greatest prize of all, a real old brass horn!   Grandad must have spent weeks in his workshop fashioning each instrument so beautifully.

Finally, from the very bottom of that wonderful sack came Grandad's own trumpet! Like the Pied Piper himself, he started playing and we all fell into line blowing our horns, or to be more precise, bellowing through them, as he guided our long winding snake up and down stairs, through the attics and even the kitchen!

Here, the holed-up ladies groaned and quickly jettisoned their teacups in favour of covering their ears as tightly as possible! Round and round we went till the old house fairly shook with the racket. How long the concert lasted I do not know, eventually we all collapsed exhausted back in the Living Room!

Seizing the momentary quiet, my mother announced that it was time to light the candles on our wonderful Christmas Tree! Exuberantly we rushed to our beautiful tree only to be set back a distance and admonished to sit very still! Of course, these were real candles, and my mother was enormously afraid of fire for she remembered a fire in the old house beams some years before which had smouldered for days before it had been discovered!

Grandad, being very, very tall, was asked to do the honours! With great solemnity, he started from the topmost candle and wound down to the very lowest! We all clapped wildly as the last candle sputtered to life and Grandad led us in the timeless old song;

"We wish you a merry Christmas, We wish you a Merry Christmas, We wish you a Merry Christmas and a Happy New Year!"

Immediately the precious candles were snuffed out (to be saved for next year) and our wonderful party was over!

Thanks to Grandad the day was saved! We basked in the glory of having given absolutely the finest party of our entire lives where even our wildest hopes and dreams had been exceeded.

ABOUT THE AUTHOR

I was born in Much Wenlock where my Ancestors have lived for Generations. My father was a farmer at the Brookhouse Farm, 1 Sheinton Street, which had been in the family since 1825. My grandfather was licensee of the George and Dragon Inn which had been in the family since 1834. Through my GG-Grandmother, Elizabeth Morrall (who married Robert Yates of Stretton Westwood in 1760), I am descended from Hugh Morrall who was bailiff for the Abbey at the time of dissolution and oversaw its closure and destruction then continued as Bailiff for the King and later owners the Abbey.

My mother was a descendant of the Preen family of Cardington and sometimes it seemed that everyone was a 'cousin' though frequently the exact connection was unknown. More recent Ancestry research has proved that our local family connections were even more widespread than I realized, and it seems we have distant cousins around the world!

I left Much Wenlock in 1960 and now live in Ontario,Canada

Some of these stories have already appeared on my 'Blog'
www.janet-preen-jones.com

Printed in Great Britain
by Amazon